T0319056

Cambridge Elements ☰

Elements in Perception
edited by
James T. Enns
The University of British Columbia

ACTION UNDERSTANDING

Angelika Lingnau
University of Regensburg

Paul Downing
Bangor University

CAMBRIDGE
UNIVERSITY PRESS

Shaftesbury Road, Cambridge CB2 8EA, United Kingdom

One Liberty Plaza, 20th Floor, New York, NY 10006, USA

477 Williamstown Road, Port Melbourne, VIC 3207, Australia

314–321, 3rd Floor, Plot 3, Splendor Forum, Jasola District Centre, New Delhi – 110025, India

103 Penang Road, #05–06/07, Visioncrest Commercial, Singapore 238467

Cambridge University Press is part of Cambridge University Press & Assessment, a department of the University of Cambridge.

We share the University's mission to contribute to society through the pursuit of education, learning and research at the highest international levels of excellence.

www.cambridge.org
Information on this title: www.cambridge.org/9781009476010

DOI: 10.1017/9781009386630

When citing this work, please include a reference to the DOI 10.1017/9781009386630

First published 2024

A catalogue record for this publication is available from the British Library.

ISBN 978-1-009-47601-0 Hardback
ISBN 978-1-009-38662-3 Paperback
ISSN 2515-0502 (online)
ISSN 2515-0499 (print)

Action Understanding

Elements in Perception

DOI: 10.1017/9781009386630
First published online: March 2024

Angelika Lingnau
University of Regensburg

Paul Downing
Bangor University

Author for correspondence: Angelika Lingnau,
Angelika.Lingnau@psychologie.uni-regensburg.de

Abstract: The human ability to effortlessly understand the actions of other people has been the focus of research in cognitive neuroscience for decades. What have we learned about this ability, and what open questions remain? In this Element, the authors address these questions by considering the kinds of information an observer may gain when viewing an action. A 'what, how, and why' framing organizes evidence and theories about the representations that support classifying an action; how the way an action is performed supports observational learning and inferences about other people; and how an actor's intentions are inferred from her actions. Further evidence shows how brain systems support action understanding, from research inspired by 'mirror neurons' and related concepts. Understanding actions from vision is a multi-faceted process that serves many behavioural goals, and is served by diverse mechanisms and brain systems.

Keywords: action recognition, mirror system, goal inferences, action observation network, observational learning

ISBNs: 9781009476010 (HB), 9781009386623 (PB), 9781009386630 (OC)
ISSNs: 2515-0502 (online), 2515-0499 (print)

Contents

1 Introduction

1.1 Motivation

Our experience of everyday social life is deeply shaped by the actions that we see others perform: consider a parent carefully watching her infant try to feed herself, a fan watching a tennis match, or a pottery student observing her teacher throw a pot. Although we may sometimes pause momentarily in puzzlement (what is my neighbour doing up there on his roof?) or be caught by surprise (by a partner's sudden romantic gesture), we normally understand others' actions quickly and without a feeling of expending much effort. By doing so, we unlock answers to important questions about the world around us: What will happen next? How could I learn to do that? How should I behave in a similar situation? What are those people like?

How, then, do we understand observed actions? The simplicity of this question, and the fluency of action understanding, obscures the complexity of the underlying mental and neural processes. To start to answer it, and in contrast to several recent valuable perspectives (e.g. Kilner, 2011; Oosterhof et al., 2013; Pitcher & Ungerleider, 2021; Tarhan & Konkle, 2020; Thompson et al., 2019; Tucciarelli et al., 2019; Wurm & Caramazza, 2021) we do not focus first on possible brain mechanisms (including the possible role of mirror neurons; see Bonini et al., 2022; Heyes & Catmur, 2022). Instead, first thinking about the problem in terms of Marr's (1982) *computational* level, we ask: why would an observer attend to the actions of others? A reasonable answer to this question might be: Observers attend others' actions to learn about the meaning and outcomes of different action kinds; to establish causal links between actors' actions and their goals, states, traits, and beliefs; and to use that learned knowledge to make predictions about the social and physical environment, and to extend one's own action repertoire. (Although beyond the focus of this review, we also sometimes attend others' actions for pure enjoyment, e.g. when watching ballet or figure skating; e.g. Christensen & Calvo-Merino, 2013; Orgs et al., 2013). Achieving these multiple complex aims requires suitable mental representations and processes – *algorithms* in Marr's (1982) terms. That is the main focus of Section 2 of this article. In Section 3, we go on to describe key neuroscientific evidence on action understanding (focusing on Marr's *implementation* level), drawing links to the concepts and constructs described in Section 2. In the final section, we identify directions for future research that are highlighted by this review.

1.2 Definitions and Scope

A survey of the literature in neuroscience, psychology, computer science, and cognitive science reveals a proliferation of terminology (action recognition, action comprehension, action identification, action perception, action observation, action interpretation, activity recognition) and equally diverse definitions. These make related, but not always consistent, assumptions and distinctions (Table 1) that may in part be due to different aspects of action that are highlighted in different experimental paradigms (Figure 1). This diversity is to be expected, given the complexity of the topic and the need to simplify it to gain traction. For this review, we adopt the term 'action understanding' as an umbrella term of convenience, to refer in general to the act of making sense of viewed human actions, and we avoid making further terminological distinctions. We resist the temptation to provide a single, concise definition of action understanding, preferring that this should emerge from the breadth of behaviours, cognitive mechanisms, and brain systems that we describe. However, some basic assumptions provide a grounding: we are concerned with observable behaviours that are intended to effect changes in the physical world or on others' minds.

What topics fall under the broad umbrella of 'action understanding'? We focus here on human action understanding, so we do not consider purely engineering-led approaches such as AI systems for what is typically known as

Table 1 Definitions of action understanding.

Gallese et al. (1996)	*'the capacity to recognize that an individual is performing an action, to differentiate this action from others analogous to it, and to use this information in order to act appropriately'*
Rizzolatti et al. (2001)	*'We understand actions when we map the visual representation of the observed action onto our **motor** representation of the same action'.*
Kohler et al. (2002), *Science*	Audio-visual mirror neurons might contribute to action understanding by evoking 'motor ideas'
Fogassi et al. (2005), *Science*	Mirror neurons selectively encode the goals of motor acts and thus facilitate action understanding
Bonini & Ferrari (2011)	*Action recognition: 'know again, recall to mind'; the ability to form a link between sensorimotor description and motor representations*
Rizzolatti & Sinigaglia (2016)	*'the outcome to which the action is directed'*

Figure 1 What we talk about when we talk about action understanding. **A:** Examples of paradigms used in the monkey literature. **B:** Examples of paradigms used in the human literature. These examples give a sense of the wide variety of stimuli and tasks used in this literature, which may include schematics, still images, animations, or movies of typical or atypical manual or whole-body actions, either in a natural or a constrained context. The diversity of these examples is matched by the diversity of terminology and definitions adopted in the action understanding literature (see Table 1).

action classification or activity recognition in that literature (Muhammad et al., 2021; Vrigkas et al., 2015). As vision is at the heart of most treatments of human action understanding, we focus on understanding seen real-world actions (but see Camponogara et al., 2017; Repp & Knoblich, 2004, for discussion of action understanding in other modalities). Evidence from animals is reviewed for its influences on thinking about human action understanding. We set aside the interpretation of actions and interactions that are conveyed symbolically, such as the decisions of a partner in an economic game like the Prisoners' Dilemma (e.g. Axelrod, 1980). Finally, we focus on understanding by typical healthy adult observers in exclusion of neuropsychological or neuropsychiatric populations. The logic for this is that while action understanding difficulties are associated with (for example) autism, schizophrenia, or semantic dementia, it is not clear that this is necessarily a central feature of those conditions (see e.g. Cappa et al., 1998; Cusack et al., 2015; Frith & Done, 1988). Action clearly is central to apraxia, however in that case definitions and diagnostics tend to focus on patients' *production* of appropriate gestures and skilled actions, particularly those relevant to tool use (Baumard & Le Gall, 2021) rather than understanding per se (but see e.g. Kalénine et al., 2010). That said, these difficulties may be informative for our thinking about the different computations and algorithms involved in action understanding; the same caveat applies to developmental evidence (Reddy & Uithol, 2016; Southgate, 2013).

Other, more specific action-related topics have recently been reviewed elsewhere: these include the perception of social interactions (McMahon & Isik, 2023; Papeo, 2020; Quadflieg & Westmoreland, 2019), the execution of joint or collaborative actions (Azaad et al., 2021; Sebanz & Knoblich, 2021), and visual perception of biological motion, especially from 'point-light' displays (Blake & Shiffrar, 2007; Thompson & Parasuraman, 2012; Troje & Basbaum, 2008).

1.3 General Principles

Two principles that have motivated many researchers' thinking about action understanding recur in our review. First, inspired by theories of hierarchies in the motor system (Georgopoulos, 1990; Harpaz et al., 2014; Turella et al., 2020; Uithol et al., 2012), actions are often described at different hierarchical levels (see Table 2). These include *kinematics* (the *how* of an action), the action *kind* (the *what* of an action), and the *intention* (the *why* of an action). These levels have strong implications for the representations and processes that are required for action understanding, and accordingly we adopt this three-way distinction to structure Section 2. The idea that actions can be described at multiple levels implies that action understanding may emphasize one of these levels over the others, depending on the observer's goals. For example, a basketball player who aims to improve his three-pointer performance might attend to the kinematics of the throw (e.g. the angle of the arm and the hand, the trajectory of the ball).

Table 2 Action understanding at different hierarchical levels.

Vallacher & Wegner (1989)	Actions can be identified on a range of different levels, from low level (how is the action performed?) to high level (why or with what is the action performed?)
Hamilton & Grafton (2007)	Muscle level (pattern of activity in all involved muscles) Kinematic level (shape of the hand, movement of the arm) Goal level (intention and outcome)
Spunt et al. (2011)	How vs What vs Why
Kilner (2011)	Kinematic level (trajectory and velocity profile) Motor level (processing and pattern of muscle activity) Goal level (immediate purpose of the action) Intention level (overall reason)
Wurm & Lingnau (2015)	Abstract level (generalization across different exemplars) Concrete level (exemplar-specific)
Thompson et al. (2019)	Action identification (e.g. precision versus whole hand) Goal identification (e.g. to grasp the cup) Intention identification (e.g. to quench thirst)
Zhuang & Lingnau (2022)	Taxonomic levels (superordinate, basic and subordinate level)

In contrast, a basketball player that aims to prevent a three-pointer by another player might attend to the intention of his opponent (e.g. by focusing on the gaze direction of the other player). This view conflicts with descriptions of action understanding as 'automatic', which would imply a process that unfolds independently of observer goals and the demands of other concurrent tasks that may 'load' cognition or perception. So in Section 2, we also describe different conceptions of automaticity and how they might play out in different action understanding situations.

Second, like any form of perception (Bar et al., 2006; De Lange et al., 2018; Hutchinson & Barrett, 2019; Rao & Ballard, 1999), action understanding enables *predictions* about what is likely to follow next, over timescales from seconds to years (Kilner et al., 2004; Oztop et al., 2005; Schultz & Frith, 2022; Umiltà et al., 2001). In some situations predictions are implicit (e.g. watching our tennis partner prepare to serve, a hunch that she will fault), and explicit in others (e.g. anticipating that the opposing tennis player will try to play a cross ball while one finds oneself in the opposite corner of the court). Predictions emerge across the hierarchical levels identified above. For example, from local cues such as hand or arm kinematics, gaze direction, and grasp preshaping, an observer can make spatially and temporally precise predictions about how an action will unfold (McDonough et al., 2019), and about the target of a reaching movement or the intended use of a grasped object (Ambrosini et al., 2011, 2015, Amoruso & Finisguierra, 2019; Amoruso & Urgesi, 2016). At the same time, our semantic knowledge about different kinds of actions includes descriptions of their typical aims, and of the kinds of events that typically tend to follow (cf. Schank & Abelson, 1977). For example, observing a friend hand-washing the dishes implies that next they will be dried and put away. Finally, observing an action supports inferences about an actor's underlying goals and beliefs, enabling predictions about what future actions would be consistent with those beliefs, or further those goals, and indeed how that actor might behave in new situations even into the distant future.

2 What, How, and Why?

2.1 'What': Two Conceptions of Action Categorization

To answer the question 'what kind of action am I seeing now?' requires extracting visual information about the surrounding scene, the actors and their movements, objects, and the relationships among those elements. This perceptual evidence must be compared to stored representations of the actions that the observer knows about. The studies considered in this section have addressed two main research questions posed by those requirements: How is long-term knowledge about action kinds organized? And how is perceptual data matched to that knowledge?

Classifying an action requires the ability to generalize over variation caused by different viewpoints, lighting effects, occlusion, and other visual variables, just as in visual object recognition (see also Perrett et al., 1989). Further, a given action (e.g. chopping vegetables) may be carried out by many possible actors, using many possible objects, in many possible locations. That problem of *generalization* is complemented by the problem of *specificity,* which requires correctly excluding from a category exemplars that do not belong. Taking an analogy from objects, for example, one must understand that a robin (canonical exemplar) and a penguin (unusual exemplar) are both birds, but that a bat, despite numerous shared features with the bird category, is not. Figure 2 illustrates that similar problems arise for action understanding, where the challenge is to correctly include visually diverse exemplars while excluding attractive foils.

Finally (and also like objects), actions are well described by taxonomies that include an abstract (or 'superordinate') level, a basic level, and a subordinate level (Rosch et al., 1976; Zhuang & Lingnau, 2022). For example, 'playing tennis' may describe an action at the basic level that is part of a superordinate

Figure 2 Successful action understanding requires generalizing over highly distinct exemplars (e.g. of <chopping vegetables>; right side) including unusual ones (centre bottom image) while excluding highly similar non-exemplars (e.g. carving; left side).

category 'sporting activities' and also includes the subordinate level 'performing a forehand volley'. The basic level has been proposed to play a key role in object categorization, e.g. as evidenced by the number of features used to describe objects, and the speed of processing (Rosch et al., 1976). Zhuang & Lingnau (2022) recently reported similar results for actions. Specifically, participants produced the highest number of features to describe actions at the basic level (see also Morris & Murphy, 1990; Rifkin, 1985). Moreover, they verified action categories faster and more accurately at the basic and the subordinate level in comparison to the superordinate level. These findings suggest that the taxonomical levels of description proposed for objects have a homology in the long-term representation of action knowledge.

Action Spaces

One major approach to understanding the representation of action knowledge was influenced by previous work investigating the mental representation of objects (e.g. Beymer & Poggio, 1996; Edelman, 1998; Gärdenfors, 2004; Kriegeskorte et al., 2008a, b). These studies develop the idea that known actions are described by multidimensional 'spaces' (see Figure 3), in which each type of action occupies a point in that space (Dima et al., 2022; Kabulska & Lingnau, 2022; Lingnau & Downing, 2015; Thornton & Tamir, 2022; Tucciarelli et al., 2019; Watson & Buxbaum, 2014; Zhuang & Lingnau, 2022). Traversing along one hypothetical dimension, actions should vary systematically on one action

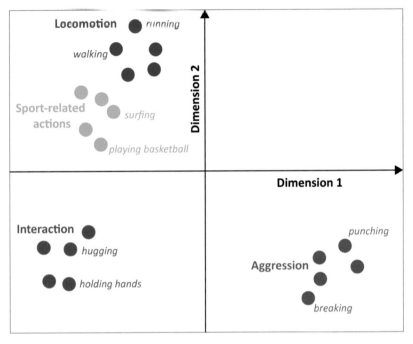

Figure 3 Illustration of the action 'spaces' idea. Action kinds may be construed as atom-like points in representational spaces, the dimensions of which may correspond to psychologically meaningful distinctions. Positions of actions reflect their values on hypothetical mental dimensions. Distances between actions are proportional to subjective judgments of the similarity between them. Here we present only a reduced example for the sake of clarity; realistic action spaces would be far more complex.

property; furthermore, by hypothesis, the distance between a pair of actions in such a space should be directly related to the perceived subjective similarity of those actions (Dima et al., 2022; Tucciarelli et al., 2019).

Several possible action spaces have been identified in studies that combine a data-driven element such as subjective similarity ratings or analyses of text corpora, with data-reduction methods such as hierarchical cluster analysis, principal component analysis, or multidimensional scaling. For example, in a series of studies based on analyses of large text corpora and other measures, Thornton & Tamir (2022) identified Abstraction, Creation, Tradition, Food, Animacy, and Spiritualism as key action dimensions (referred to as the ACT-FASTaxonomy). These dimensions successfully captured variance in the judged similarity of action words, and also described the socially relevant features of actions (e.g. how, why and by whom an action is performed).

Focusing instead on action images, Tucciarelli et al. (2019) required participants to group pictures of actions by their perceived similarity in a multi-item arrangement task (Kriegeskorte & Mur, 2012). Analysis by k-means clustering and principal component analysis revealed several meaningful action categories, including food-related actions, communicative actions, and locomotion. These categories fell along dimensions that were organized according to the type of change induced by the action, and the type of need to be fulfilled by the action (e.g. basic/physiological versus higher social needs). Kabulska & Lingnau (2022) used a very similar approach with pictures of 100 different actions that revealed additional action categories such as Interaction, Gestures, and Aggressive actions. Analyses of action features provided evidence for a strong dimension capturing the positive or negative valence of the action. Still further evidence shows how typically intended outcomes may also shape action spaces. For example, Tarhan et al. (2021) analysed data from a multi-arrangement task to find that a goal similarity model predicted judgments of action similarity better than models based on movement similarity or on visual similarity.

Together, this family of approaches has revealed a diverse set of candidate principles and dimensions that organize action knowledge. The 'spaces' that emerge from a given study depend on the kinds of actions being considered, and the specific task set for the observers (a topic that we will return to in Section 3). It may be that multiple distinct spaces, or hierarchically nested spaces, best capture the huge and diverse range of actions that observers can understand, rather than a single space. Indeed, in each of the studies described, a large proportion of variability remained unexplained, suggesting that there are additional organizing principles not yet identified.

Our knowledge about actions changes as we learn; and in different contexts, different aspects of actions may be more or less immediately relevant. Accordingly, action spaces are likely to be dynamic over both short and long time scales. Attention or context effects may dynamically 'warp' the shape of action spaces as they are used in making action judgments. For example, Shahdloo et al. (2022) used neuroimaging to reveal how the distributed patterns of activity evoked by actions were modulated by changing the observers' immediate task to attend either to their communicative or their locomotion characteristics. At longer time scales, effects of experience and expertise are relevant. For one example, over the course of years of practice, a gymnast must build a dense and detailed 'space' representing her specialist events, which would likely have more, and more meaningful dimensions relative to a novice observer. Moreover, attention and experience might modify the weights of specific dimensions (Gärdenfors, 2004). To our knowledge, these ideas have not been explored empirically from the action spaces perspective.

By definition, the organization of observed actions into action spaces shows similarities with semantic networks (e.g. Collins & Quillian, 1969) and semantic categories generally (see e.g. Levin, 1993; Pinker, 1989; Talmy, 1985). However, the organization of actions depicted by visual stimuli and by verbal material is bound to differ in important ways since visually presented actions are concrete instantiations of a specific action, whereas language has the flexibility to refer to actions at varying levels of abstraction. For related discussions, see Tucciarelli et al. (2019); Vinson & Vigliocco (2008); and Watson & Buxbaum (2014).

Action Frames

The 'space' metaphor is very powerful for capturing the key dimensions of action knowledge as well as subjective judgments of the similarity of different kinds of action. One limitation of the approach, however, is that it obscures some of the rich internal structure that constitutes our knowledge of familiar actions. This is not easily captured in a dimensional representation that treats action concepts as single points in a mental space. Accordingly, building on previous conceptions of knowledge frames (Minsky, 1975) and scripts (Bower et al., 1979; Schank & Abelson, 1977) here we consider the idea of *action frames*. Related ideas have also been more recently explored in the context of action understanding (Aksoy et al., 2017; Chersi et al., 2011; Zacks et al., 2007), although these have tended to focus more narrowly on specific issues such as the sequential nature of actions. An action frame may be seen as a schematic representation that describes, abstractly, important features of an action, such as its intended outcomes or goals; means by which the goals typically are achieved; and the kinds of movements, postures, objects, and locations associated with that kind of action (Figure 4). These associations are assumed to be picked up from statistical co-occurrences in our natural environment. Action frames may help to identify action kinds by interacting with the output of perceptual systems that recognize objects and scenes (Epstein & Baker, 2019), detect and classify people (Pitcher & Ungerleider, 2021), and estimate their poses and movements (Giese & Poggio, 2003). These perceptual systems analyse an observed action, abstracting over some details (e.g. the colour of a knife) while emphasizing others (e.g. its position relative to the ingredients, and its motion related to the movements of the chef). Consistent evidence gathered in the perceptual systems and schematic action frame representations mutually reinforce each other, whereas inconsistent evidence leads to suppression. Recent perspectives have also highlighted the perceptual significance of typical relationships amongst scene elements (Bach et al., 2005; Green & Hummel, 2006; Hafri & Firestone, 2021; Kaiser et al., 2019), which will also have diagnostic value for distinguishing among different kinds of

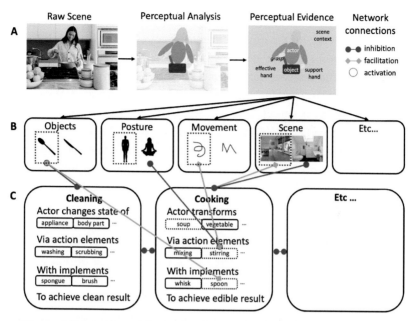

Figure 4 Illustration of the 'action frames' perspective. **A, B:** Perceptual subsystems process objects, body postures, movements, and scenes to extract relevant aspects of the action, and the relationships among them. **C:** Mental 'action frames' capture the roles, relationships, and reasons that comprise our action knowledge. Slots of a given frame gather perceptual evidence about scene elements. Matches increase the evidence for one action (<cooking>) relative to others (<cleaning>). Normally, interactions between perceptual subsystems and action frames cohere rapidly to select one action frame; action understanding is this convergence of activity. Links omitted for clarity.

actions. We can understand action classification as emerging from competitive interactions amongst perceptual systems, and between perceptual systems and action frames, such that (normally) this system rapidly converges on an interpretation that best coheres with the available evidence (cf. Ernst, 2006; Netanyahu et al., 2021).

Action frames must be abstract enough to encompass the wide perceptual variety of different action instances that we described earlier. They must also be flexible or probabilistic, rather than rigid, to account for our ability to tolerate variations: for example, cooking normally happens in the kitchen but may also take place outdoors in a campsite. Further, a key aspect of our knowledge about action kinds is an understanding of the desired outcomes that normally motivate a given action. Accordingly, frames need to describe not only knowledge about the directly observable elements that constitute an action; they also need to include descriptions of the expected mental states of the actors. Finally, they also require access to more general semantic knowledge of the physical and social world. This includes, for example, knowledge about typical cause-and-effect relationships (cooking pasta makes it soft and edible; stealing from someone makes them angry). Likewise, we deploy knowledge about the ways in which the properties of objects like tools make them suited to specific kinds of manipulations for specific kinds of outcomes – the shape, hardness, and weight distribution of a hammer makes it useful for driving in nails (e.g. Buxbaum et al., 2014; Osiurak & Badets, 2016; see also Binkofski & Buxbaum, 2013).

Action frames as described here might offer several useful properties. First, they may describe the highly predictable way in which actions generally unfold over time that is not readily captured by a semantic space of actions. For example, purchasing food ingredients is not just semantically related to cooking; one typically precedes the other in a predictable way. Likewise, at a finer grain, preparing a soup may include obtaining, washing, peeling, and slicing vegetables, sub-actions that only make sense in a specific order. These regularities enable an observer to anticipate what is likely to follow next (Aksoy et al., 2017; Chersi et al., 2011; Schank & Abelson, 1977; Zacks et al., 2007). It may be difficult to capture these kinds of relationships in a scheme in which action kinds are considered as 'points' in a multidimensional Euclidean space. A more abstract and compositional representation may be better suited to capture the temporal and causal relationships that describe typical chains of actions.

Prediction

We previously highlighted the important theme of prediction in action understanding. Here we briefly explore how expectations and predictions might play out from the perspectives of action spaces and action frames. For one example, Tamir, Thornton, and colleagues have proposed that the proximity of actions in a space reflects not only semantic similarity, but also transitional probability. In general, one cooking event is more likely to immediately follow another cooking action than (say) a vehicle-repair action. In a series of studies, Thornton & Tamir (2021a) found that participants' ratings of transition probabilities between actions corresponded well to actual rates of action transitions (determined on the basis of several large naturalistic datasets). More important, Thornton & Tamir (2021b) demonstrated that actions that were close to each other in the ACT-FAST action space described above were also more likely to follow each other.

From the action frames perspective, expectations – for example, evidence that an action will unfold in a kitchen – allows relevant action frames (e.g. for cooking, eating, and washing up) to compete with and suppress less relevant ones. In turn, this enables pre-activation of cooking-relevant objects (e.g. a knife), again at the expense of other unrelated objects (e.g. pliers). The net effect of these competitive interactions should be a relative advantage in understanding actions that are consistent with expectations, by suppression of unlikely alternatives. Indeed, when actions are embedded in an incongruent context, they take longer to be processed in comparison to actions embedded in a neutral or congruent context (Wurm & Schubotz, 2012, 2017). Likewise, ambiguous actions are recognized with higher accuracy when taking place in a congruent context in comparison to incongruent or neutral contexts (Wurm & Schubotz, 2017; Wurm et al., 2017a). Here, the surrounding context (e.g. the emotional facial expression of an agent) shapes the interpretation of the action (e.g. an approaching fist with the intention to punch or to greet the observer with a fist bump; see e.g. Kroczek et al., 2021), just as ambiguous objects (e.g. Brandman & Peelen, 2017) and emotional facial expressions (Aviezer et al., 2012) are interpreted in reference to their immediate context in the domains of scene and body perception.

To summarize, here we have considered two complementary perspectives on how the mind organizes long-term knowledge about familiar actions. These are not mutually exclusive ideas: as action understanding is so complex, each perspective may better describe different aspects of what we know about actions, how that knowledge is applied to understanding 'what' a given action is, and how that supports predictions about the actors and events that we interact with.

2.2 'How': Observational Learning, Imitation, and Expertise

In many contexts, the specific manner in which an action is carried out ('how') may be more immediately relevant than its category ('what'), so here the action frames and spaces constructs may have fewer applications. Much of the research under this heading has focused on learning, to ask how observing actions can change the observer's own action repertoire; and conversely, how one's own experience with a family of actions influences how those actions are perceived. We also describe a strand of the literature in which attending to the 'how' of an action provides the observer with cues about the beliefs, intentions, or longstanding traits of the actors.

Observational Learning

Observational learning (sometimes 'social learning') refers, in the broadest sense, to acquiring knowledge about the contingencies between behaviour and outcomes by observing others (Bandura & Walters, 1977). By observation, without the need for first-hand experience that may be ineffective, slow, or even dangerous, we can learn that touching an electrified fence is painful; that others find playing a musical instrument rewarding; or that posting controversial opinions to Twitter attracts both praise and condemnation.

One focus area within this broad theme concerns the transfer of learning from one domain (normally vision) to motor performance. What can we learn about serving a tennis ball, shaping a clay pot, or performing brain surgery, by watching an expert do those things? A fundamental issue in this literature concerns the role of symbolic or cognitive representations in mediating the benefits of observational learning. As an example, a tennis novice observing a coach in order to learn to serve might try to segment the observed movement according to summary cues such as 'down together', 'up together', 'back', 'hit', and 'follow-through'. In a classic study of motor sequence learning, Bandura & Jeffrey (1973) compared participants' learning and retention of simple manual action sequences as a function of rehearsal type. Those participants who were instructed to encode observed sequences in verbal terms (e.g. with letter codes) recalled sequences better than those who were not, especially over longer intervals. The insight is that at least in some cases, symbolic representations are more informationally compact and durable (Uithol et al., 2012), and therefore more readily rehearsed and retrieved at a later time, compared to 'raw' motor representations.

Related research asks whether the action representations acquired from observation are explicit, in the sense of being overtly retrievable and usable as part of a strategy, or instead implicit, in the sense of being acquired without awareness. For example, serial response tasks require participants to rapidly press one of several keys corresponding to the location of a single target. Typically, if the sequence of locations is repeated in a second-order cycle, response times improve with practice. However, explicit knowledge of the sequence may be absent, for example as tested in a subsequent task requiring participants to guess the next item in a series (Seger, 1997). In contrast, studies of observational learning – in which participants learned keypress sequences simply by watching the target events appear – found that sequence learning was mediated mainly by explicit, verbalizable knowledge (Kelly et al., 2003). Interestingly, Bird & colleagues (2005) found that when sequences were observed not simply as visual events, but as the outcomes of a live actor's behaviour, implicit learning was also revealed, suggesting that the actor's presence encouraged a more first-person like encoding of the action sequences.

The preceding examples all relate to categorical actions and action sequences – pressing one of four keys, for example – for which the specific action dynamics were not relevant. Other studies have examined observational learning with actions that involve more continuous variables. For example, Mattar & Gribble (2005) required participants to make simple reaches under the influence of an unseen 'force field' that deflected those movements. Participants who first watched another actor perform this task before attempting it showed stable benefits (e.g. smaller disruptions to their own reach trajectories) compared to controls. Notably, this observational learning remained essentially intact even when it took place under a demanding concurrent cognitive load, suggesting a relatively automatic and implicit form of learning (see also Section 3).

Conversely, other work has examined the transfer of motor learning to visual action judgments. Casile & Giese (2006) demonstrated how learning to perform an unusual pattern of walking movements selectively improved visual detection of those movements when they were rendered as point-light animations. In a more naturalistic context, Aglioti et al. (2008) demonstrated that experienced basketball players made better predictions about the outcome of observed free throws in comparison to individuals with similar visual experience (experienced coaches, sports journalists) and to novices. Improved performance of players in this example, compared to experienced coaches, invites the interpretation that motor experience specifically contributes to improved action understanding. In a similar vein, Knoblich & Flach (2001) found that participants were better able to judge from a video where a thrown dart would land, when that video depicted a previous throw that they had performed themselves, compared to another thrower. An important feature of each of these motor-to-vision studies is that the observed actions were seen from a side view, that is, one that is normally unavailable for one's own actions. Therefore, the learning exhibited in those situations must extend over modalities (from motor to visual) and must also generalize across visual perspective.

The preceding findings imply a close overlap between an observer's own motor repertoire and her ability to understand actions. Yet other findings show that these two variables can be dissociated. For example, a series of studies of individuals with congenital dysplasia who lack upper arms (and therefore have no upper-limb motor representations), revealed essentially normal performance in a variety of tasks. These included different aspects of action understanding, including the ability to name pantomimes and point-light animations, to learn new actions, and to predict the outcome of basketball free-throws (Vannuscorps & Caramazza, 2016; but see Vannuscorps & Caramazza, 2023). Developmental studies reveal similar dissociations; for example, three-month-old infants have been shown to interpret observed actions as goal-directed before they are able to perform reach and grasp actions themselves (Liu et al., 2019; see also

Southgate, 2013). In sum, whereas several studies suggest that the ability to
detect subtle differences in the kinematics of observed movements is modified
by the observer's experience, relevant motor experience is not always
a necessary requirement for the ability to understand actions.

Imitation

Observational learning generally relates to the effects of experience on later
performance (or perception) of an action. In contrast, imitation concerns the
attempt to immediately replicate another person's action. Here, key research
questions have concerned the development of imitation (to what extent is
imitation present from birth?) and automaticity (e.g. to what extent does imitation occur in spite of the observers' current goals?).

   The claim that even newborn infants possess not only the ability to imitate
facial expressions but a tendency to do so spontaneously (Meltzoff & Moore,
1977) has been highly influential, although the core findings have been ques-
tioned by more recent large-scale replication efforts (e.g. Oostenbroek et al.,
2016). Similarly, evidence for 'automatic' imitation in adults has proven fruitful. A simple procedure, typically called the *automatic imitation task,* was
developed by Brass and colleagues (Brass et al., 2000; Cracco et al., 2018).
Here, participants lift either their index or middle finger in response to a visually
presented numeric cue. At the same time as the cue, an on-screen hand is shown
to lift either the index or middle finger. While the finger movement is task-
irrelevant, participants are nonetheless normally faster when that movement
also matches the action they are required to execute, compared to when it does
not match. Variants of this procedure have been developed to understand this
compatibility effect, to identify its neural correlates (Darda & Ramsey, 2019), to
assess its malleability following training (Catmur et al., 2007), and to test the
claim that it is 'automatic' (Cracco et al., 2018).

   In contrast to these relatively simple and controlled tasks, researchers in
social psychology have asked whether, in more naturalistic settings, participants
tend to unwittingly mimic the movements or body postures of confederates. For
example, Chartrand & Bargh (1999) reported a 'chameleon effect' whereby
individuals may unintentionally match others' overt behaviours, and moreover
that the experience of being imitated in this fashion increases liking. In general,
then, there is some evidence of the tendency for irrelevant or incidental actions
of others to influence the observer's own concurrent behaviours, even in the
absence of an explicit goal to imitate.

   A final important distinction is that between imitation and emulation, where
the latter refers to an achievement of the same end state via different specific

motoric means (see also Bekkering et al., 2000; Csibra, 2008; Heyes, 2001; Tomasello et al., 1993). For example, given no specific instructions, preschool children will tend to emulate the target of an action (e.g. reaching for the right ear) instead of producing a faithful copy of the observed action (e.g. reaching for the right ear with the contralateral hand; Bekkering et al., 2000). This finding illustrates that actions may normally be understood by default from the 'intentional stance' – as deliberate and rational behaviours, performed by an agent for a reason – a topic we return to in Section 2.3.

'How' beyond Observational Learning

The specific manner in which an action is performed (e.g. grasping a bottle at the top or the bottom) can provide cues about the immediate goal of an actor (e.g. to move the bottle or to use it to pour a drink). Observers may use a variety of sources, such as the kinematics and the preshaping of the hand, as well as perceived gaze direction (e.g. Aglioti et al., 2008; Ambrosini et al., 2011; Cavallo et al., 2016) to anticipate how an action will unfold, and to coordinate actions of two or more actors (see also Azaad et al., 2021). Access to the precise way in which an action is performed also plays a role in the predictive coding framework of action understanding (Kilner, 2011; Kilner et al., 2007). We will return to this point in Section 4.

Studies from the direct perception tradition (Gibson, 1979/2014) and more recently from the social vision framework (Adams et al., 2011) examine how the observed patterns of others' movements provide rich clues about the states and traits of other individuals (with the caveat that such cues may not be fully valid). For example, studies of point-light recordings of actors performing simple actions revealed that they support above-chance identification of the actor (Loula et al., 2005) and discrimination of emotion (Atkinson et al., 2004), gender (Kozlowski & Cutting, 1977), or sexuality (Johnson et al., 2007). Those studies guided by the direct perception framework have tried to identify simple physical properties of movement patterns that reliably cue social variables without the need for complex cognitive analysis. For example, Kozlowski & Cutting (1977) identified that a lower centre of movement reliably signals female as opposed to male actors from walking patterns. Studies in the related social vision framework have tended to focus on outcomes, as seen, for example, in the finding that observers' judgments of actors' health from movement patterns was a reliable predictor of which actor would be selected in a hypothetical political election (Kramer et al., 2010). In sum, the details of action dynamics, even from minimal stimuli like 'point-light' animations, can provide information about the states and traits of the actors that perform those actions. In the following section, we examine how observed actions also provide evidence about more complex mental states such as goals and beliefs.

2.3 'Why': Intentions, Mental States, and Traits of Observed Actors

A meaningless waggle of the hands, or a flag waving in the wind, are not actions: actions are carried out with the intent to effect a change in the state of the world. As described in Section 2.1, typical outcomes are an essential part of our general, abstract semantic knowledge about different action kinds. Here, we explore the situation in which an observer understands the goals of a specific actor undertaking a specific instance of an action. To emphasize the distinction: it is one thing to know that, in general, cleaning the kitchen is an action intended to reduce the amount of dirt in that room, and another to understand the behaviour of a specific individual performing specific movements in a specific kitchen with a broom and dustpan.

As noted in Section 1, understanding the goal or desired outcome of an action is sometimes regarded as the pinnacle of a hierarchical encoding of that action. Yet the 'why' behind an action may often be described at multiple levels: Why is he moving the broom forward and backward? Because he knows that this is an effective way to gather dust. Why is he sweeping? Because he desires the end-state of a clean floor. Why is he cleaning the floor? Because he wants his expected visitors to judge him positively. Furthermore, the goals of the *observer* will influence the level at which she seeks to identify the actor's intentions (Bach et al., 2007; Spunt & Lieberman, 2014; Thompson & Parasuraman, 2012; Thompson et al., 2023). As an example, an observer might have the goal to imitate for the sake of learning; to figure out whether the other person needs help; or to form a first impression. What is common across all of these levels, however, is that the observer normally treats the actor with the *intentional stance* (Dennett, 1987). That is, when watching the man sweep his kitchen, she attributes to him mental states such as knowledge, beliefs, and goals – all of which may well differ from her own. She will understand these mental states as having a causal role in his decisions about what actions to perform and how; and conversely, she will expect that his actions follow rationally from his beliefs and goals, given his available repertoire.

Framed in these terms, we can examine some of the main approaches to revealing how observers understand the intentions of a specific actor from a specific observed action. In one approach (e.g. Brass et al., 2007; de Lange et al., 2008; Dungan et al., 2016; for a meta analysis, see van Overwalle, 2009), actions are presented that are unusual or unfamiliar in some aspect: for example, a person switching on a light with her knee (which makes sense if the hands of the actor are occupied, but not if they are empty). The error signals that are generated by such unusual actions would normally trigger a search for an explanation, just as would be expected for other violations of expectations (such as seeing a rowboat in a desert landscape; Brandmann & Peelen, 2017; Oliva & Torralba, 2007). Generally, when there is a significant mismatch between a percept and one's expectations or action knowledge, a more explicit and effortful process is engaged to understand the action. To what extent does that search involve representing the actor's mental states?

One approach to examining mental state attribution in action understanding is by reverse inference[1] from the activity of brain regions that are thought to support such 'mentalizing', as revealed in false-belief or perspective-taking tasks (e.g. Saxe & Kanwisher, 2003; Schurz et al., 2014). Unusual actions (switching on a light with the knee) recruit such brain regions more when they are presented in an implausible context (actor's hands are free) relative to a more plausible context (the hands are otherwise occupied; Brass et al., 2007). The logic is that the implausible action elicits an attempt to identify an account of the situation, which by default is one that relies on representing the mental states of the actor.

A related topic in social psychology (e.g. Ambady & Rosenthal, 1992; Estes, 1938; Tamir & Thornton, 2018) concerns how action understanding provides cues about the states and traits of an actor (Bach & Schenke, 2017). Here we are concerned with the meaning and outcomes of the action, rather than the dynamics as reviewed in Section *'How' beyond Observational Learning*. For example, observing an actor make a donation to a charity supports general predictions about his future behaviour in related situations (such as helping an old person cross the road), perhaps mediated by a guess about his personality traits. Indeed, the fundamental attribution error (Gilbert & Malone, 1995; Ross, 2018) reveals how observers tend to emphasize explanations of other people's behaviour in terms of the actor's personality traits, often neglecting the contribution of the situation or context. For example, having observed that a colleague regularly drives his car instead of his bike to work despite a relatively short distance, we might consider him lazy, without taking into account that he might have to drop his children at a more distant nursery on his way to work. These concepts and findings

---

[1] Applied to neuroimaging, 'reverse inference' describes estimating the cognitive processes involved in a task on the basis of the brain regions that are engaged by that task (in fMRI, for example). While sometimes used perjoratively, reverse inference may be a strong form of induction where the activity of the region in question is consistently selective across different contexts (Poldrack, 2006).

reveal how action understanding contributes to general processes of person perception in the social-psychological sense.

Finally, several authors have adopted a Bayesian inverse planning approach to model how mental state inferences are drawn from observed actions (e.g. Baker et al., 2009; Baker et al., 2017). As an example, Baker et al. (2009) presented human observers with simple animations consisting of an agent moving through a two-dimensional environment with obstacles and target locations. The animations stopped at a predefined point in time, and participants had to report which target they thought the agent was trying to reach. The authors modelled causal relations between the environment, goals, and actions in the form of rational probabilistic planning in Markov decision problems. To infer the agent's belief and goals from their actions, this relation is inverted using Bayes' rule. The goal of the agent is to achieve a specific state of the environment, and this goal can change over time and can have varying levels of complexity. The authors observed that participants' judgements could be well predicted on the basis of these Bayesian inverse planning models. Whereas the paradigm focused on spatial navigation, similar models can also be adapted to more complex, naturalistic tasks. In sum, the contribution of this modelling approach is to formalize ideas about how observed variables (actions) may be used to make inference about unobservable variables (actors' beliefs and goals).

To briefly summarize Section 2: we have so far reviewed different perspectives on action understanding, asking what kinds of mental representations and processes might be used to understand an action. What emerges clearly is that the answer depends on the goals of the observer: action understanding is not monolithic. While there are important examples that cross the boundaries, the tasks of classifying an action, understanding how an action is carried out, and understanding the intentions of the actors, draw on different mental capacities. Broadly, classifying actions requires a rich semantic 'database' of our long-term knowledge about actions; attention to the means by which an action is performed implicates implicit, motoric knowledge as well; and adopting the intentional stance to make inferences about others' mental states requires implicit theories of how traits, states, intentions, and behaviour interact.

3 Attention and Automaticity

3.1 Varieties of Attention

Do observers automatically understand an action that they observe, as sometimes suggested (Ferrari et al., 2009; Iacoboni, 2009; see also Cook et al., 2014, for a review)? The evidence reviewed in Section 2 already indicates the limits of the automaticity of action understanding, given its multifaceted nature, and its dependence on distinct processes as well as contextual factors including the observer's own experience and goals. To focus more closely on the question, here we consider several conceptions of automaticity that have been put forward in the social cognition literature (Bargh, 1989). To simplify the discussion, in each case we refer to examples that have used the 'automatic imitation' task (Brass et al., 2000; see above) as a proxy measure of understanding a simple viewed movement.

First, what aspects of action understanding proceed even when they are not relevant to the task at hand? Say the observer is trying to find a friend who is performing on a crowded stage; to what extent does he also represent the performer's actions even though these are not relevant to his goal? In the context of the automatic imitation task, Hemed et al. (2021) approached this issue by including incompatible finger movements that were also never task relevant (and so not part of the participants' response set). Such irrelevant movements did not affect task performance, providing one example of the attentional filtering of action even in a very minimalistic setting. In other words, there is a limit to the automaticity of processing even simple movements viewed in isolation.

Second, what aspects of action understanding are resistant to top-down control, which is to say they are carried out even when the observer deliberately tries not to do so? Chong et al. (2009) reported that the 'automatic imitation' of a viewed grasping action (measured via response compatibility effects) was eliminated when participants' attention was directed to another object presented at the same location. Here, again we see evidence against strong 'automaticity' in the finding that even a single, foveated action will affect the observer's behaviour less to the extent that it is not in the focus of selective attention.

Third, to what extent does action understanding persist in a complex visual environment, or under increased mental load? For example, in daily life, an action may be observed in a serene setting (watching the only other patient in a dentist's waiting room) or in a complex one (watching fans in a sporting arena). At the same time, one may be free of distraction, or alternatively heavily distracted by another ongoing mental task (e.g. attending an online meeting while also home-schooling). These examples highlight the dimensions of perceptual and cognitive load, which deeply affect everyday cognition (Lavie & Dalton, 2014). Several recent studies have explored the effects of perceptual load (Catmur, 2016; Thompson et al., 2023) and cognitive load (Ramsey et al., 2019) on tasks that require either explicit action category judgments or measure action perception implicitly (but see Benoni, 2018). The general strategy is to assess how an action task is impacted by a second concurrent task, performed at low versus high load. In perceptual tasks, load is typically manipulated by adding more, or more varied, stimulus items along with the task-relevant item. Cognitive load may be varied by requiring participants to maintain one versus many letters or digits in working memory. Catmur (2016) reported that perceptual load amplifies the effects of irrelevant finger movements in the automatic imitation task. In contrast, Ramsey et al. (2019) reported no effects of concurrent cognitive load on the strength of the automatic imitation effect. This was the case even when the items to be maintained in working memory (images of hand postures) were highly similar to the automatic imitation cues. Findings like these help establish the automaticity of action understanding with respect to other ongoing perceptual and cognitive processes.

The studies discussed in this section all focused on relatively simple finger movements within the automatic imitation paradigm. Other studies have tested different action understanding tasks, along with manipulations to examine the relative automaticity of action processing and its modulation by perceptual and cognitive load (Lingnau & Petris, 2013; Spunt & Liebermann, 2014).

3.2 Task Set and Observer Goals

Observers may actively try to attend to the kinematics of an action (perhaps to learn how to improve one's tennis backhand), its category (is that backhand a slice shot or not?), or its intended result (is that a drop shot or a long volley?). These distinct kinds of attentional sets in turn have an impact on more basic perceptual processes that analyse the scene: in the first example, perhaps attention is focused on the movements of the arm, whereas the angle of the racket may be more relevant in the second example. This intention to select aspects of the action may fail, in the sense that there may be processing of irrelevant aspects of the action as well. For one example, on the principles of object-based attention (Cavanagh et al., 2023), attempting to focus on the movement of the arm may necessarily entail selection of the tennis racket it holds as well. Similarly, based on neuroimaging studies, Spunt & Lieberman (2013) have suggested that focusing attention on 'why' an action is executed also elicits a representation of 'how' it is executed, even if the latter is not task relevant.

Finally, attention is sometimes construed as the selection of internal representations or templates, for example to support visual search for a certain target item such as a face or house (Chun et al., 2011; Peelen & Kastner, 2014; Serences et al., 2004). Applied to actions, we can think about search templates in the frameworks of action spaces and action frames (Section 2.1). In terms of action spaces, attention might 'reshape' representational geometries (see also Edelman, 1998; Kriegeskorte & Kievit, 2013; Nosofsky et al., 1986). As an example, attending closely to the location in which an action takes place (e.g. a kitchen) might effectively 'expand' the representational space of kitchen-related actions, and 'compress' the space around other actions (see also Nastase et al., 2017; Shahdloo et al., 2022; Wurm & Schubotz, 2012, 2017). In this metaphor, 'expanding' dimensions of a representational space implies enhancing distinctions that are relevant to that dimension (e.g. amongst different kinds of slicing, chopping, and grating) and de-emphasizing other distinctions that are not relevant (Figure 5). In contrast, in terms of action frames, attention might facilitate or inhibit the connections between different scene elements (cf. Figure 4B) or between different action frames (Figure 4C), again to highlight those that are contextually relevant.

To briefly summarize Section 3: while we argue that a general answer to the question 'is action understanding automatic' must be 'no', much remains to be learned about how different senses of automaticity apply to different contexts. We suggest that the concepts and approaches developed in the study of visual attention in general, are well suited to test assumptions about the representations captured in action spaces and action frames. This broader approach, we suggest, will be more fruitful than seeking a simple answer to the question of whether or not action understanding proceeds automatically.

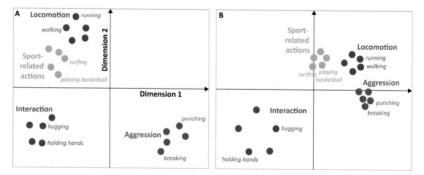

Figure 5 Schematic illustrating expansion and compression of action spaces via attention. **A:** Action space of four hypothetical action categories without attention (see also Figure 3). **B:** Action space of four hypothetical action categories while attending to the category highlighted in red. In this example, distinctions among the members of the attended category are enhanced, whereas distinctions within irrelevant action categories, and also between action categories, are attenuated.

4 Brain Mechanisms

In the preceding sections, we focused on the mental processes and representations that enable action understanding. Next, we review evidence and theories about the brain regions, networks, and distributed patterns of activity that support action understanding tasks. Neuroscientific studies in this area have been very strongly influenced by the discovery of the 'mirror neuron' and related theoretical views on the contribution of the motor system to visual action understanding. Accordingly, we structure this section roughly chronologically to track initial findings and conceptions of mirror neurons, following subsequent waves of human neuroimaging and non-human primate studies, and finally to consider more recently emerging theoretical perspectives. Specifically, we start our journey in Section 4.1 by briefly reviewing evidence for visual action-selective neurons in the macaque superior temporal sulcus (STS). We then review in Section 4.2 the initial reports and key findings about 'mirror neurons' in macaque premotor cortex. Section 4.3 reviews studies inspired by those findings that sought signatures of a human 'mirror neuron system'. These have used several methods to probe the activity of motor regions in visual action understanding tasks, and to identify potential markers of 'mirror-like' representations. More recently, as we see in Section 4.4, several groups have turned away from the emphasis on motor representations, to instead draw methodological and theoretical parallels between action understanding and research on visual object perception. Finally, in Section 4.5, we come full circle to consider more recent discoveries about mirror neurons in the macaque, and to review how thinking has evolved about possible alternative functional roles of mirror neurons or a mirror 'system' in human action understanding. Throughout, we highlight points of contact between neuroscientific findings and concepts, and the themes introduced in Sections 2 and 3. Figure 6 provides a visual guide to some of the regions in the human and the macaque brain that we discuss.

4.1 High-Level Visual Representations of Actions in the Macaque

Perrett and colleagues demonstrated that macaque STS contains neurons that selectively respond to different types of observed manual actions, such as picking, tearing, or rotating (e.g. Perrett et al., 1989). Some of these neurons generalized over different instances (e.g. front versus side view), and also were sensitive to agent-object interaction (e.g. a hand manipulating fur versus a hand performing the same action but with a gap between hand and fur). From findings like these, the authors concluded that networks of neurons within the STS collectively represent socially significant aspects of others' movements and postures, such as their direction of attention, or their intention to act.

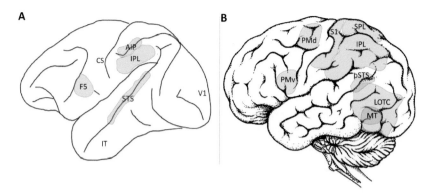

Figure 6 Key brain regions discussed in Section 4. **A: Macaque brain, lateral view**. Adapted from Riley & Constantinidis (2016). **B: Human brain, lateral view**. Adapted from https://www.supercoloring.com/coloring-pages/human-brain-anatomy. F5: rostral portion of ventral premotor cortex, CS: central sulcus, AIP: anterior intraparietal area, IPL: inferior parietal lobe, STS: superior temporal sulcus, IT: inferior-temporal cortex, V1: primary visual cortex, PMv: ventral premotor cortex, PMd: dorsal premotor cortex, IFG: inferior frontal gyrus, S1: primary somatosensory cortex, SPL: superior parietal lobule, pSTS: posterior superior temporal sulcus, LOTC: lateral occipitotemporal cortex, MT: middle temporal area.

Later, action sensitive neurons with more complex properties were discovered in the same general region. As mentioned earlier, under natural conditions intentional grasping actions in humans are accompanied by an anticipatory gaze shift of the actor towards the object (Ambrosini et al., 2011, 2015; Flanagan & Johansson, 2003). Neurons in macaque STS have been shown to detect subtle variations in this relationship. For example, Jellema et al. (2000) found stronger responses in anterior STS neurons when both a reaching movement and gaze were directed towards the monkey, in comparison to a reach towards the monkey accompanied by a shift of gaze somewhere else. Findings like these have been taken as evidence of neural computations that support discriminating intentional actions from unintentional movements.

4.2 Initial Discovery and Characterization of Mirror Neurons

Macaque ventral premotor area F5 was long known to contain neurons that discharge during the execution of specific object-directed hand actions (e.g. Rizzolatti et al., 1981, 1988), and during the observation of objects that require a specific grip type (Murata et al., 1997; Rizzolatti et al., 1981). Other studies also showed selectivity in these neurons for object-directed actions, irrespective of the effector involved (e.g. grasping food with the hand or the mouth; Rizzolatti et al., 1988). In a further study of this region, Di Pellegrino et al. (1992) incidentally observed that some F5 neurons also discharged during the passive observation of certain actions (e.g. picking up food) performed by the experimenter. Further observations with other actions revealed a direct correspondence between the effective action during observation and execution in a subset of all examined neurons (12 out of 184). Later studies identified additional properties of these 'mirror neurons': for example, that they would only discharge during an interaction between an actor and an object (Gallese et al., 1996), and that they sometimes responded to expected but occluded grasping actions (Umiltà et al., 2001). Furthermore, visuo-motor neurons found in the monkey inferior parietal lobule (IPL) were sensitive to the target of otherwise similar manual actions (e.g. grasping to place food into a container next to the shoulder versus grasping to place food into the mouth; Fogassi et al., 2005; see also Bonini et al., 2010). Further reviews of these and other early key studies are found in Kilner & Lemon (2013).

Modern perspectives on the relationship between perception, decision-making, action planning, and action execution tend to emphasize shared representations (e.g. common coding framework; Prinz, 1997), and describe these as cascading parallel processes rather than serial stages (e.g. Cisek, 2007). Mirror neurons, because they discharge during the observation and execution of similar actions, have been proposed to provide the neural basis of such shared representations. As we will show in the following, this view has evolved and expanded greatly as new findings have emerged (for related reviews, see Kilner & Lemon (2013), Rizzolatti & Sinigaglia (2016), Heyes & Catmur (2022), and Bonini et al. (2022)).

Based on the initial discovery of mirror neurons, Di Pellegrino et al. (1992) concluded that premotor cortex not only retrieves appropriate motor acts in response to sensory stimuli (such as the shape and size of objects), but also in response to the meaning of the motor acts of another individual. In other words, the authors argued that these neurons provide an explicit representation of the link between the execution of a motor act and its visual appearance when performed by another individual (Di Pellegrino et al., 1992). Gallese et al. (1996) went further to propose that mirror neurons play a role in action understanding of motor events, which they defined as 'the capacity to recognize that an individual is performing an action, to differentiate this action from others analogous to it, and to use this information in order to act appropriately'. In line with the division between the ventral and dorsal pathways (Goodale & Milner, 1992; Ungerleider & Mishkin, 1982), the authors argued that neurons in STS might provide an initial description of hand-object interactions and capture a semantic (or 'What') representation of the action, whereas mirror neurons in F5 might provide a match with the 'motor vocabulary', capturing a pragmatic (or 'How') representation of actions.

Based on the observation that mirror neurons respond to hidden actions, Umiltà et al. (2001) further reasoned that mirror neurons have the capability to *infer* both the action and the object from past perceptual history, and suggested that the hidden condition requires *cognitive effort* from the monkey since it must *pay attention* to the actions of the experimenter and *'reconstruct the missing part of the action'* (page 161). These key points – italics ours –contrast with earlier proposals that mirror neuron activity supports 'automatic' action understanding (see also Cook et al., 2014).

Following the observation that some mirror neurons in monkey inferior parietal cortex code the target of an action, Fogassi et al. (2005) argued that individual motor acts are combined by means of 'intentional chains' which allow the observer to predict the goal of the action, and from that to *'read the intention'* of the actor. This is a proposal about the discovery of internal mental states from observed actions, as discussed in Section 2. As a form of 'direct perception', it stands in contrast to the mentalizing or 'theory of mind' perspective, by which goals would be understood via inferences about beliefs and other mental states. Most starkly, some researchers (e.g. Rizzolatti et al., 2001) have claimed that actions are understood 'when we map the visual representation of the observed action onto our motor representation of the same action', without 'inferential processing' or 'high-level mental processes' – and that mirror neurons constitute the basis for this understanding. Note the contrast between this perspective and the descriptions of action spaces and action frames (Section 2), which describe our rich semantic knowledge about actions that is not obviously motoric in nature.

Claims that mirror neurons constitute a solution to the problem of action understanding, and that this takes place automatically, have remained controversial. For example, single cell recordings are correlational, so they do not allow inferences regarding a causal role of measured neurons in the tasks under investigation (see also Caramazza et al., 2014; Hickok et al., 2009; Thompson et al., 2019). So it remains unknown whether mirror neurons play a causal role in action understanding in the macaque, a problem that is exacerbated because identifying suitable tasks and measures of 'understanding' in non-human primates is not trivial. Moreover, for practical reasons, studies of mirror neurons have focused on immediate reach-to-grasp movements targeting food or other desirable objects in most cases. It is therefore not clear how these kinds of findings generalize to the wide repertoire of actions (see also Sliwa & Freiwald, 2017) performed with various body parts, objects and tools in human daily life.

We return in Section 4.5 to more elaborate arguments and debates about the role of mirror neurons. First, however, we review key points in the large literature on human observers that has been directly inspired by the discovery of mirror neurons and by the initial ideas about their possible functional roles.

4.3 A Human Mirror System?

Whereas it is not straightforward to identify and characterize mirror neurons in humans directly, several indirect approaches have been developed to identify mechanisms that link observed and executed actions in the human brain (Figure 7). In each case, the core of the logic is that there should be some neural signature that is sensitive to the match between a specific performed action, and observation of that same action.

Physiological Measures of Motor System Activity

One way to examine the level of activation of the motor system is to induce a brief electrical current in the primary motor cortex via transcranial magnetic stimulation (TMS). This can trigger measurable **motor evoked potentials** (MEPs) in contralateral peripheral muscles such as in the hand. The strength of these MEPs indexes the excitability of the corresponding stimulated motor region (for a review, see Bestmann & Krakauer, 2015). Moreover, the comparison of MEPs between different muscles of the hand that are involved in specific types of grasping movements enables an examination of muscle-specific activation of the motor cortex during action observation. In general, findings that the excitability of the motor cortex can be modulated by passively observed compatible actions have been taken as evidence of a 'mirror-like' mechanism in humans (Rizzolatti et al., 2001).

Using this approach, several studies found that observing manual grasping actions leads to a muscle-specific activation of some of the same motor pathways that would be used if the observer were to perform that action (Baldissera et al., 2001; Fadiga et al., 1995; Maeda et al., 2002; Strafella & Paus, 2000). Such findings have been interpreted as a sign of an automatic 'resonance' in the observer's motor system caused by observing the action. Other studies demonstrated that MEPs are sensitive to predicted action outcomes. For example, Aglioti et al. (2008) found that in expert basketball players, specific MEPs were evoked during the observation of missed free-throws, upon release of the ball but before the outcome was known (see also Gangitano et al., 2001, 2004; Kilner et al., 2004). More recent studies demonstrated that MEPs are not only modulated by low level kinematic features of an action, but are also affected by higher level processes, such as the difference between honest and deceptive

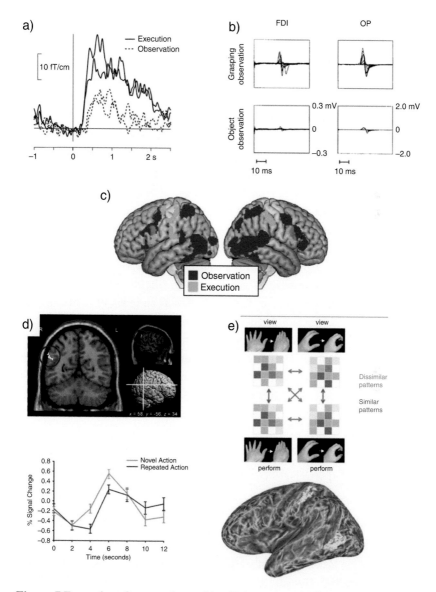

Figure 7 Examples of approaches to identifying aspects of human brain activity that share properties in common with the mirror neuron. **A:** Post-stimulus 'rebound' of the suppressed cortical mu-rhythm response following execution of a repetitive action (solid lines) or passive observation of a similar action (dotted lines). From Hari et al., 2006. **B:** Enhancement of the contralateral Motor-Evoked Potential by passive observation of a grasping action (top) relative to an object observation control (bottom) in two hand muscles (first dorsal interosseus, left; opponens policis, right). From Fadiga et al., 1995.

actions (Finisguerra et al., 2018) or the congruence between the context and the action (Amoruso & Urgesi, 2016; Betti et al., 2022). Findings like these have contributed to a debate about whether MEPs reflect an automatic motor resonance, or whether instead they are also modulated by top-down influences (for a review, see Amoruso & Finisguerra, 2019).

Another series of experiments exploited the **mu rhythm**, a frequency in the cortical EEG signal in the range of 8–13 Hz over sensorimotor cortex. In general terms, the mu rhythm is suppressed during selective attention and motor preparation, and the mu rhythm can be sensitive to the type of movement and handedness (for review, see Hobson & Bishop, 2007). Mu suppression, like MEPs, has been used as an index of motor system activity during the passive observation of others' actions. In common with the properties ascribed to some mirror neurons, for example, suppression of the mu rhythm is stronger during the observation of a precision grip of an object compared to a mimicked precision grip in the absence of an object (e.g. Muthukumaraswamy et al., 2004a, b). However, the view of the mu rhythm as an index of human mirror neuron activity also remains debated (e.g. Hobson & Bishop, 2017). In particular, it is not straightforward to determine whether a suppression in the 8–13 Hz window originates from sensorimotor areas, or whether it instead stems from a modulation of the alpha rhythm originating from occipital cortex. This alternative indicates that the modulation of the mu rhythm during action observation might instead, or additionally, reflect visual attention or perceptual processes.

Studies from the brain stimulation and mu rhythm lines of work have been useful to explore how the states of the observers' motor system are influenced

---

Caption for Figure 7 (cont.)

C: Human brain regions commonly activated in action observation, in action execution tasks, or by both tasks, in fMRI experiments. From Hardwick et al., 2018. **D:** Top: Human IPL exhibits repetition suppression for transitive hand actions that were mimed and then observed. From Chong et al., 2009. Bottom: Reduction in the hemodynamic response function to repeated actions relative to non-repeated actions. From Chong et al., 2009. **E:** Top: Schematic illustration of the logic from multivoxel pattern analysis (MVPA) fMRI studies that sought to identify regions in which local voxel patterns are more similar for the same action than different actions, across performance and observation. Bottom: Brain regions that exhibit the similarity patterns described in the top panel, as revealed by surface-based MVPA of fMRI data. From Oosterhof et al., 2010, 2013.

by what the observer sees and understands about an action. However, the functional implications of some of these findings remain debated, in that several interpretations remain about what processes these neural measures reveal.

Human Neuroimaging

Early human neuroimaging studies using PET (Grafton et al., 1996; Rizzolatti et al., 1996) and fMRI (Iacoboni et al., 1999) adopted the logic that anatomical overlap between brain areas that are recruited during the observation of actions, and the execution, imagination, or imitation of actions, would provide evidence of 'mirror-like' human brain representations. Some common findings in these initial studies laid the foundation for later human neuroimaging investigations. For example, fMRI studies demonstrated that during passive observation of goal-directed actions, participants recruit a consistent set of brain region including the ventral premotor cortex (PMv) extending into the posterior IFG, the preSMA, somatosensory cortex, anterior and superior sections of the parietal cortex, and portions of the lateral occipitotemporal cortex (see Figure 7B). As a shorthand, these regions are often collectively referred to as the 'action observation network'. Later studies showed how parts of this network (premotor, parietal, and somatosensory areas) also overlap with the areas involved during motor imagery and/or movement execution (for meta analyses, see e.g. Arioli & Canessa, 2019; Caspers et al., 2010; Hardwick et al., 2018; but see Turella et al., 2009). Together, findings like these have been taken to show a common neural representation of the corresponding visual and motor aspects of actions, as a possible system-level homologue of the mirror neuron.

However, an influential commentary by Dinstein et al. (2008) noted limitations in this logic, namely that spatially overlapping activations (e.g. of regions responding to observed and to executed actions) may reflect overlapping but distinct neural populations rather than a shared representation (see also Peelen & Downing, 2007). Better evidence for a 'mirror like' representation would be found in a demonstration that neuronal populations within overlapping regions are selective for specific motor acts. Accordingly, several studies have investigated cross-modal action selectivity using fMRI adaptation or repetition suppression (e.g. Grill-Spector & Malach, 2001). This method is based on the observation that the repetition of a specific stimulus property, such as object category, leads to an attenuation of the fMRI signal in neuronal populations that represent the repeated stimulus property.

Several studies followed this approach to seek evidence for cross-modal action selectivity as suggested by Dinstein et al. (2008). Neuronal populations with such properties should adapt when the same action is repeated, across performance or observation of that action, compared to different actions. Dinstein et al. (2007) and Press et al. (2012) obtained action selective adaptation during observation and also during execution in overlapping parietal regions. However, they did not observe cross-modal adaptation – that is, for observation of an action followed by its execution, or vice versa. Chong et al. (2008) found cross-modal adaptation in the right IPL, but only tested for execution followed by observation (see also de la Rosa et al., 2016). In contrast, Lingnau et al. (2009) tested for cross-modal adaptation in both directions; this effect was found in the left IPL, but only when observation was followed by execution. Finally, using a similar approach, Kilner et al. (2009) found cross-modal adaptation in the IFG in both directions.

Following these initial contradictory results, doubts arose about one of the key assumptions underlying these studies: namely, that mirror neurons adapt to repetition in the same way as other types of neurons. Caggiano et al. (2013) reported that mirror neurons in F5 do not reduce their response amplitude following two repetitions. By contrast, Kilner, Kraskow, & Lemon (2014) found a modulation of the firing rate, the latency, and beta band power of the local field potential in this region, but only after repetitions of 7–10 trials.

Together, human neuroimaging studies using repetition suppression to examine cross-modal action selectivity remain inconclusive. It is likely that at least one contribution to this is the variety of tasks, stimuli, and action types that have been tested. For example, the combined effects of action type (e.g. object-directed vs intransitive), viewpoint (e.g. first- or third-person), and meaningfulness (e.g. simple movements vs grasps vs pantomimes) have not been factorially explored within a single repetition suppression study of action understanding.

Multivoxel pattern analysis (MVPA; Norman et al., 2006) approaches offer another way to identify shared visual and motor representations of actions that may avoid the issues with interpreting 'overlap' identified by Dinstein (2008). For example, in a series of studies, Oosterhof et al. (2010, 2012a, b; reviewed in Oosterhof et al., 2013) used whole-brain surface-based 'searchlight' MVPA (Kriegeskorte et al., 2006; Oosterhof et al., 2010) to identify brain regions in which the local patterns of activity are a) similar for a given action, whether passively observed or performed by the participant; and also b) dissimilar for different actions. This logic captures the core concept of the mirror neuron in carrying representations that generalize over modality and also distinguish between different actions. These studies consistently revealed regions of the anterior parietal and lateral occipitotemporal cortex that met those defining criteria. Further, patterns of activity in the ventral premotor cortex were also cross-modal and action specific, but only for actions viewed from the first-person perspective – in contrast to initial evidence on mirror neurons that exhibited at least some evidence for selectivity to third-person views of action (see also Caggiano et al., 2011). By contrast, viewpoint independence of cross-modal action-selective representations was obtained in parietal and occipitotemporal cortex only (Oosterhof et al., 2012a).

Finally, the most direct way to examine whether the human brain contains cells with mirror properties is to perform direct recordings in humans undergoing preparation for neurosurgery. Mukamel et al. (2010) recorded extracellular single and multiunit activity from a group of neurons in patients being treated for epilepsy. The authors found neurons that responded both during observation and execution of actions in the supplementary motor area, the hippocampus, and other nearby regions. A subset of these neurons showed excitation during execution, but inhibition during observation (see also Kraskov et al., 2009). The presence of both excitation and inhibition is in line with computational models of action planning (see e.g. Cisek, 2007) that assume that several potential actions are specified in parallel and compete with each other until there is enough sensory evidence in favour of one of these actions.

The preceding section has briefly laid out some of the main neuroscientific approaches that have been used to apply the mirror neuron logic to the human brain. Overall, the results of these studies converge to implicate several key regions in one or more aspects of action understanding (see Figure 6). Where they diverge is in the extent to which they confirm or fail to confirm the key concepts of cross-modal, view-invariant, and action-specific representations that were inherited from initial descriptions of mirror neurons.

Expertise

If one's own motor representations play a causal role in action understanding, it stands to reason that the richness of those representations should influence the nature of understanding. Accordingly, several studies have examined how different kinds and levels of action expertise (and specifically motor expertise) change the way these actions are processed in brain regions of the action observation network. The general logic is that relative to the novice, an expert's richer motor representations of an action repertoire enable an improved, or even qualitatively different, understanding of observed actions from that domain.

Observers' expertise modulates fMRI activity within the action observation network (see Turella et al., 2013, for a review). For example, one series of studies examined brain responses of expert dancers from two disciplines (ballet and capoeira). In their domain of expertise, dancers exhibited more activity in prefrontal and parietal regions relative to dance movements of the other domain

(Calvo-Merino et al., 2005) and to dance movements of the expert domain that were motorically but not visually familiar (Calvo-Merino et al., 2006; see also Cross et al., 2006, and Jola et al., 2012). The interpretation of these findings was that motoric aspects of dance expertise influenced the way that experts visually perceived and understood actions, by way of a cross-modal visuo-motor representation.

An apparent paradox in this literature is that in some cases the effect of experience appears to decrease rather than increase the activity in action observation regions (see e.g. Gardner et al., 2017). For example, Petrini et al. (2011) found such a pattern of results when comparing the neural activity elicited by observing 'point light' animations of drumming actions, in experienced versus novice drummers. These divergent effects may reflect two different facets of expertise: on the one hand, expertise (e.g. with performing a class of actions) provides a rich framework by which observed actions may be assigned meanings that are not accessible to novices; hence a relative increase in activity in relevant regions for experts. In contrast, expertise also entails familiarity with actions from the relevant domain, supporting an improved ability to predict what will be seen next. Indeed, the literature on perceptual expectations emphasizes the suppressing effect of expectations on neural activity in line with predictive coding models (Summerfield et al., 2008).

Modulation by Task Requirements

In Section 3, we discussed the automaticity of action understanding. Neuroscientific studies have also approached this question by asking to what extent brain activity is modulated by manipulations of the observers' task, such as by instruction to attend to an action or instead to an object in a scene (Wurm et al., 2015); to attend to the goal or to the effector involved in an action (Lingnau & Petris, 2013); to attend to the type of action performed by an animal or rather its taxonomic category (Nastase et al., 2017; see also Kemmerer, 2021); or to attend to the type of action, the actor, or the colour of the object (Orban et al., 2019).

Here, typically the task modulates the engagement of specific brain regions implicated in action understanding. For example, one study showed a higher response in the lateral occipitotemporal cortex when focusing on the 'what' of an action, and a higher response when focusing on the 'why' of an action in several areas, including the dorsomedial prefrontal cortex and the temporal pole (Spunt et al., 2011; but see Spunt et al., 2016). Part of the logic of such studies is to apply reverse inference from previous findings. For example, activity in the 'action observation network' may be interpreted as evidence for processing the 'how' of an action (Rizzolatti & Craighero, 2004; Rizzolatti & Sinigaglia, 2010; Caspers et al., 2010), whereas activity in regions linked to mentalizing tasks is taken to reveal an effort to understand the intentions behind an action ('why'; e.g. van Overvalle, 2009; van Overvalle & Baetens, 2009). More generally, these studies reinforce the view discussed in Section 3, namely that action understanding is not reflex-like, but rather recruits neural processes that adapt to serve the observer's current goals.

4.4 Parallels with Object Vision

Alongside the studies that have focused on describing possible human homologues of mirror neurons, other researchers have increasingly adapted research questions and methods from the domain of object recognition to action understanding. These parallels include, for example: how are invariant representations achieved over viewpoints, or over different exemplars (Figure 2)? What are the critical features and dimensions underlying the encoding of actions? And what are the temporal dynamics of the brain's extraction of those features? Here we briefly summarize some recent work in this area.

Generalization and Abstraction

Which brain regions show selectivity for specific observed actions, and how abstract or generalized are those representations? Initially, motivated by findings from the mirror-neuron literature, many studies used region-of-interest (ROI) approaches to focus on regions such as the PMv and the IPL. To establish whether these regions demonstrate action selectivity – a response that can distinguish between different observed actions – several studies relied on fMRI adaptation. For example, Hamilton & Grafton (2006) reported that the anterior IPS encodes the object that is the target of the reach, in a way that generalizes over the specific trajectory that is required to reach that object. Similarly, Hamilton & Grafton (2008) reported a representation of the outcome of an action (e.g. an opened or closed box) that generalizes over the specific kinematics required to achieve that outcome, in the right IPL, the left aIPS and the right IFG (see also Majdandžić et al., 2009). Finally, using a related approach called TMS adaptation, Cattaneo et al. (2010) adapted participants to the observation of hand or foot actions manipulating an object. TMS applied to the IPL and the PMv led to shorter response times for repeated actions relative to non-repeated ones, irrespective of the effector. By contrast, TMS applied to the STS revealed effector-specific adaptation, suggesting action representations at different hierarchical levels in the STS and the IPL/PMv. Together, these studies are a good early example of how neuroimaging and brain stimulation methods could answer qualitative questions about levels of neural action representation, and how they vary across different brain regions.

Tests of the abstractness of an action representation have also been addressed with a cross-decoding MVPA approach. Here, a classifier might initially be trained to distinguish between two observed actions (A and B), based on the activity patterns within a given brain region. Next, that classifier is tested to see whether it can still distinguish between the two actions following a variation in the way the actor performed the action. Using this logic with a whole-brain searchlight approach, several studies reported that it is possible to decode observed actions from patterns of activity in the lateral occipitotemporal cortex (LOTC) and in the IPL across different target objects (Wurm et al., 2015) and across objects and the kinematics required to manipulate these objects (Wurm & Lingnau, 2015). Similarly, Hafri, Trueswell, & Epstein (2017) were able to distinguish between different interaction categories (e.g. biting, kicking, slapping) across different visual formats (static images versus dynamic videos) based on activity in several regions, including occipitotemporal, parietal and left premotor cortex. And Wurm & Caramazza (2019) were able to decode actions from videos to written descriptions and *vice versa* from activation patterns in human LOTC.

Together, what these MVPA decoding findings show is that distributed activity patterns can reveal rich information about viewed actions that go beyond a literal description of a single instance of an action, to extend to more general properties. One important point of focus in this body of work has been around the anatomical regions implicated. As noted, the initial human neuroimaging work focused on the role of ventrolateral frontal and parietal regions. However, a typical pattern in a growing number of more recent human studies (e.g. Oosterhof et al., 2012; Wurm & Lingnau, 2015; Wurm et al., 2015, 2017b) is that these abstract action representations are instead found more consistently in posterior occipitotemporal regions. In part, this discrepancy may reflect different neural distributions in different regions, which may be more or less visible to MVPA. Indeed, by using single-cell recordings from two tetraplegic patients with electrode arrays in the posterior parietal cortex, Aflalo et al. (2020) were able to decode manipulative actions across different stimulus formats in human parietal cortex.

The studies reviewed in this section so far clearly indicate how rich information about observed actions is implicit in the activity patterns seen in human brain regions beyond the core motor system. Indeed, a common pattern over multiple studies is that the highest degree of generalization, in common with object vision, is found in higher-level visual areas and the parietal cortex (see e.g. Ayzenberg & Behrmann, 2022).

Organization of Observed Actions in Space and Time

In Section 2.1, we described the logic of multidimensional 'spaces' that could describe some aspects of knowledge about action categories. More recent studies have adapted this logic – which emerged from work on the representations of concepts, objects, and faces (Gärdenfors, 2004; Shepard, 1958; Valentine et al., 2016) – to examine how patterns of brain activity might describe similar neural 'spaces' for action representation. Many of these studies adopt the representational similarity analysis (RSA) approach, which uses measures of similarity to describe the notional geometry of a representation of a class of events or stimuli (Kriegeskorte et al., 2008a). In this way, comparisons between behavioural and neural measures, or between two different neural measures, are possible at a level of abstraction above the specific items. For example, Tucciarelli et al. (2019; see also Tarhan et al., 2021; Zhuang et al., 2023) compared representational geometries based on the perceived semantic similarity of observed actions from behavioural measurements, with geometries derived from fMRI multi-voxel activity patterns. They found that neural activity patterns in a set of regions along the ventral and dorsal stream resembled the behaviourally determined action space, in the sense that there was a significant positive relationship between the 'space' inferred from behavioural judgments, and that determined from the patterns of brain activity. Thus, these approaches can link, at an abstract level, subjective and neural representations of action knowledge.

If patterns of neural activity capture action 'spaces', what is the organization of these spaces? Tarhan & Konkle (2020) identified five distinct distributed clusters of brain regions covering the lateral and ventral occipitotemporal cortex and the intraparietal sulcus. These carried information about body parts and the target of an action during the passive observation of short naturalistic video clips. Responses in four of the identified clusters were organized by the spatial scale of the action (e.g. from small, precise movements involving the hands to large movements involving the entire body). Using a similar approach, Thornton & Tamir (2022) were able to decode amongst observed actions on the basis of their six-dimensional ACT-FAST taxonomy, based on fMRI activity measured from a widespread set of occipitotemporal, parietal and frontal regions. Finally, using EEG during passive observation of short video clips depicting everyday actions in combination with behavioural ratings, Dima et al. (2022) observed a temporal gradient in action representations. Over a period from 60 to 800 ms, the shape of action 'spaces' changed from an emphasis on visual features, to action-related features, and then to social-affective features. Together, studies like these show how specific action-space models can be developed and tested on the basis of neuroimaging data.

Multiple studies have found particularly strong evidence that LOTC plays a role in representing action spaces. For example, Tucciarelli et al. (2019) found that patterns of activity across the LOTC best capture the semantic similarity structure of observed actions, when variability due to specific action features such as body parts, scenes, and objects is removed. In that study, actions related to locomotion, communication, and food formed clusters both in the behaviourally determined and in the neural action space. Given evidence for abstract action 'spaces' in LOTC, is there evidence of any anatomical organization to the patterns of activity within this region? We have previously made the case for representational gradients across the LOTC, such that the way it encodes an action property (e.g. the extent to which it is person or object-directed) varies continuously across the region. Specific proposed gradients include a posterior-anterior gradient for the dimensions concrete-abstract and visual-multimodal, and a dorsal-ventral gradient for the dimensions intentional-perceptual and animate versus inanimate (e.g. Papeo et al., 2019; Tarhan et al., 2021; Wurm et al., 2017b; for reviews, see Lingnau & Downing, 2015; Wurm & Caramazza, 2022).

Together, this family of findings shows that the representational similarity approach can test hypotheses about how action knowledge is captured in distributed patterns of brain activity. Moreover, these studies have highlighted the role of the LOTC, and point to several action-relevant features that are captured in this region. At the same time, this review highlights that there is not yet consensus on a single set of organizing dimensions. Indeed, given the flexibility with which observers can process an action depending on their attentional state or task set, such a consensus may not be expected.

4.5 Mirror Neurons Revisited

Rizzolatti & Sinigaglia (2010) argued that while other people's actions could, in principle, be perceived on the basis of visual processing, such a description lacks an understanding 'from the inside as a motor possibility', which was instead proposed to be provided by mirror neurons. Since then, following their discovery and initial characterization, additional properties of mirror neurons have been revealed that continue to shape ideas about how they contribute to action understanding. These findings have highlighted several complex factors that influence, or are even a core part of, action understanding. They take us further away from thinking of action understanding as a direct mapping of 'the visual representation of the observed action onto our motor representation of the same action' (Rizzolatti et al., 2001) or the idea that actions are understood 'without inferential processing' or 'high-level mental processes' (Rizzolatti & Fogassi, 2014; Rizzolatti & Sinigaglia, 2010). Here, we review some of that newer evidence, and then go on to describe more recent perspectives that extend beyond the idea of mirroring in action understanding.

A key family of findings is that mirror neuron responses are in some cases influenced by contextual factors. As an example, Csibra (2008) pointed out that the reach-to-place and the reach-to-eat conditions used in the study by Fogassi et al. (2005) differed with respect to the object (food versus non-food) and the presence or absence of a container. The role of context is also explicitly highlighted in a computational model for the execution and recognition of action sequences proposed by Chersi et al. (2011). Likewise, several studies demonstrated a distinction between *peripersonal and extrapersonal space* (Caggiano et al., 2009; Maranesi et al., 2017) and the *subjective value* of an object that is the target of an action (Caggiano et al., 2012). Further, some F5 mirror neurons are sensitive to the difference between visual stimuli that either caused or did not cause an action (e.g. a hand, represented as a disc, reaching, holding and moving an object, compared to a control condition with a similar movement pattern in which the disc made no contact with the object; Caggiano et al., 2016). This difference was obtained for naturalistic stimuli, and also for abstract stimuli depicting the same causal (or non-causal) relationships, suggesting a broader role in understanding events beyond observed motor behaviours.

Further, some mirror neurons have properties that suggest they form a representation of an upcoming action based on the action affordances that an object presents (Bonini et al., 2014; see also Bach et al., 2014). ('Affordances' refer to aspects of an object that are closely linked to a particular kind of action, such as the handles of objects such as pans or mugs.) This class of so-called 'canonical' mirror neurons discharges both during an observed action (e.g. grasping a large cone with a whole hand grip) and during the presentation of an object for which that same grip would be appropriate (e.g. a large cone). Further, the firing rate of the majority of such neurons is suppressed when the object is presented behind a transparent plastic barrier (Bonini et al., 2014), suggesting that these neurons only fire when it is actually possible for the monkey to interact with the object. This pattern of findings implies a pragmatic coding of an observed object by mirror neurons, in the sense that the representation is influenced by context and the potential for an overt action. While this observation does not necessarily apply to all mirror neurons, it does strongly imply that mirror neuron activity may at least in part support the preparation to act on an object, in contrast to contributing to a more receptive understanding process.

Together, findings like these highlight the contribution of the object, the context and the potential to perform an action in shaping mirror neuron activity, in line with a network-level approach to action understanding (see also Bonini et al., 2022). Inspired by findings like these, and by other theoretical considerations, several authors have addressed the possible contributions of the mirror neuron system from a broader perspective; we discuss these next. Note that these proposals, like the original studies on mirror neurons, tend to focus on manual actions performed on a single object, so their applicability to a wider range of actions requires further investigation (see also Section 5).

Csibra (2008) proposed that mirror neurons might play a role in action reconstruction instead of direct matching. Similar to the steps involved in object recognition, where mid-level features are assembled into objects (e.g. Brincat & Connor, 2004; Güçlü & van Gerven, 2015; Kravitz et al., 2013; Tanaka, 1997; Yau et al., 2013), the proposal is that visual analysis can translate mid-level features such as movements and body parts into complete action representations (see also Fleischer et al., 2013; Lanzilotto et al., 2020; Perrett et al., 1989; Wurm et al., 2017b). Csibra (2008) furthermore argues that if observed actions are interpreted at a relatively abstract level in the visual system, the resulting representation can serve as the input to the motor system, where these actions can be reproduced. In this view, the role of mirror neurons would be to help an observer to reconstruct the motor programs required to perform such observed actions (for similar arguments, see Bach et al., 2014; Kilner, 2011). Thus, the action reconstruction proposal posits a role for mirror neurons not as the initial or sole route to action understanding, but rather as an intermediate step between primarily visual encoding and the retrieval of relevant motor behaviours ('perception-for-action'; see also Maranesi et al., 2017). This interpretation is compatible with the observation that the activation of canonical mirror neurons is suppressed when a plastic barrier prevents the monkey from manipulating the object (Bonini et al., 2014). Such an intermediate step supports an observer in coordinating their own actions, and with engaging in joint actions (cf. Azaad et al., 2021).

In contrast to viewing the mirror neuron system as a strict feedforward recognition system, several authors have proposed predictive coding models of the mirror neuron system (Donnarumma et al., 2017; Kilner, 2011; Kilner et al., 2007; Oztop et al., 2005; Oztop et al.,2013; Wilson & Knoblich, 2005). In general, predictive coding is the idea that the brain constantly generates and updates mental models, each of which tries to predict representations at the next lower processing level. In this framework, backward connections that compare the prediction to the obtained representation are used to compute a prediction error, which the system tries to minimize. Applying this framework to the mirror neuron system, Kilner (2011) proposed that the most likely goal of an action is derived from a visual analysis of the context of the action (in particular, the target object). Ventral stream areas including the middle temporal gyrus and the anterior portion of the IFG are proposed to retrieve actions that are semantically associated with this object, whereas medial regions of the IFG select the most appropriate action. In turn, the motor parameters corresponding to the selected action are retrieved by mirror neurons on the posterior IFG. On this view, the sensory consequences of actions are fed back to the ventral stream via dorsal regions of the action observation network where the predicted sensory consequences are compared with the observed sensory information. The neural representations of the likely sensory causes of the action are adjusted until the mismatch between the predicted sensory consequences and the observed sensory information is minimized (see also Oztop et al., 2005). Here, then, 'understanding' the action constitutes a reverse inference of the intent from what is observed. In line with this view, a recent depth-resolved ultra high-field fMRI study comparing feedback signals arriving in parietal cortex reported a higher signal during the observation of predictable versus scrambled sequences (Cerliani et al., 2022). In sum, predictive coding provides a biologically plausible mechanism that might describe an alternative role for mirror neurons during action observation (namely, the prediction of sensory consequences of the most likely action), and that can explain a number of findings that are hard to reconcile with a strict feedforward account of the mirror neuron system (see also Oztop et al., 2013).

Finally, in a recent review, Orban et al. (2021) highlight the role of parietal area AIP in integrating different types of visual information (body movements, body-object relationship, and action-related object features) along with haptic feedback. The authors draw a connection to the *affordance competition hypothesis* (Cisek, 2007) which describes a model of action preparation and execution. In contrast to the assumption of serial processing stages consisting of sensory processing, decision-making and movement planning, this view proposes that sensory processing includes, in parallel, an analysis of the action possibilities, which compete with each other until enough evidence is collected in favour of one of these options. Orban et al. (2021) argue that, similar to the concept of object affordances, parietal neurons code the affordances of an observed action ('social affordances'). According to this proposal, visuo-motor parietal neurons code observed actions, such as grasping, and action classes, such as kinds of object manipulation. In turn, these are linked to associated motor plans for the selection and planning of potential motor actions in response to the observed action. Thus, in contrast to the special roles originally attributed to mirror neurons, the proposal by Orban et al. (2021) highlights the convergence of various different types of visual, somatosensory, and proprioceptive information in parietal cortex, which both helps to identify an observed action, and to support context-appropriate movement planning.

In sum, these recent findings and theoretical proposals suggest ways in which mirror neurons are more complex than originally conceived, and further are

embedded in a wider network of brain areas, some of which are more special
ized for a visual analysis of the observed action. Collectively, these developments reduce the focus on mirror neurons per se as providing a unified, abstract
representation of actions at the pinnacle of an action understanding system.
What emerges instead is a view of mirror neurons operating as part of a wider
set of processes in which they may provide a concrete representation of
observed actions that is closely related to the preparation of corresponding
motor plans.

5 Directions for Future Research

Our review points to many open questions. Here we highlight a few, following
the structure of the preceding sections.

Both the action frames and action space perspectives (Section 2) require
further development. As an example, there is more to learn about how action
spaces develop and change with experience. Developmental studies as well
as studies with specific populations might provide valuable insights into these
questions. Moreover, we need to better understand the structure underlying
the representational spaces of actions, and how they are influenced by current
task goals. Hypothetical action spaces amount to a proposal about dimension
reduction, collapsing many observations into a simpler structure. However,
depending on the algorithms used to reduce the dimensionality of the data, we
might arrive at very different kinds of structures. A recent computational
approach offers a method by which such principles might be discovered,
bottom-up, in neural or behavioural data (Kemp & Tenenbaum, 2008).
Likewise, we need to better understand how action frames organize action
knowledge, and how they are acquired – another topic that would profit from
developmental studies, as well as from studies with special populations (such
as neurological patients, or experts in specific types of actions). There are
some initial findings on how information about an action is extracted and
elaborated over time, particularly from an action spaces perspective (e.g.
Dima et al., 2022), but this requires further investigation. Finally, some action
categories might have processing 'priority' over others, on the basis of being
more related to survival over an evolutionary time frame (e.g. attacking,
eating) than others that are more recent (e.g. reading; see also Cisek, 2019).
This relates to similar previous proposals about, for example, emotional face
expressions, direct eye gaze, and fear-inducing objects such as snakes. The
methods applied to those topics could be extended to learn more about highly
salient action kinds.

While the action spaces perspective has proved productive in generating hypotheses about patterns of activity in human neuroimaging studies, this is less straightforward from the action frames view. Given the conceptual similarity with abstract knowledge schemas, we might expect to find similar brain networks engaged, such as the ventromedial prefrontal cortex and the hippocampus (Gilboa & Marlatte, 2017). Measures of functional connectivity, or of connectivity patterns (e.g. Anzelotti & Coutanche, 2018; Anzelotti et al., 2017) could be used to seek evidence of the predicted interplay between regions involved in action observation, object recognition, body and face perception, and scene perception. A better understanding of this interplay would also provide a basis for examining how these dynamics are shaped by the observer's action understanding goals.

The research to date on the effects of attention and perceptual or cognitive load on action understanding has focused on a fairly limited set of tasks that could be expanded in further studies. In parallel, as the brain encoding of action knowledge becomes better understood (such as in pattern classification studies of the LOTC), this creates opportunities to use multivariate approaches to measure action representations to see how they are modulated under different attention and load conditions.

To date, much of the human neuroscientific work on action understanding has used correlational measures such as fMRI or EEG. Perturbation methods such as TMS allow the targeted disruption of one or more brain regions, as a way to index their normal contributions to behavioural action understanding tasks. That approach has mainly been applied to motor regions, and to quite simple action observation tasks (see also Section 4). Yet more recent work implicating parietal and occipitotemporal regions in rich action knowledge points to further targets for intervention, and predictions about how disrupting those regions should impact on action understanding behaviours.

Biologically inspired models of action understanding have been developed to explain manual reaching and grasping (e.g. Fleischer et al., 2013) and have been inspired by predictive coding and Bayesian modelling (e.g. Bach & Schenke, 2017; Baker et al., 2009; Kilner et al., 2007; Oztop et al., 2005). Extending this line of research towards a wider range of actions while incorporating the rich sources of information that are known to contribute to processing the 'What, How and Why' of actions would be fruitful for the generation of new testable hypotheses. More specifically, potential lines for this modelling work will be to more explicitly incorporate (a) the role of information obtained about actions from different perceptual systems that analyse objects, scenes, postures and movements and the way this information is combined; and (b) the observer's own knowledge about how a family of actions is performed, such as through first-hand experience with a particular sport.

The cognitive neuroscience of object understanding has been transformed in recent years by the use of deep neural network models (Cadieu et al., 2014; Cichy & Kaiser, 2019; Spoerer et al., 2017). These have been proposed to offer a source of hypotheses about the transformations that link early visual encoding of a visual scene (edges, surfaces, contours, etc.) and later high-level object representations (see also Güçlü & van Gerven, 2015; Seeliger et al., 2021). Similarly, the layers of such networks have been compared to stages of the inferotemporal pathways of the visual brain (although such comparisons are not necessarily straightforward; Bowers et al., 2022). It may be worthwhile to explore whether we can identify similarities between the processing hierarchy and critical features for actions captured in the visual system, and deep neural networks that are trained on action understanding tasks. Additional insights might be gained from synthesizing images that are expected to strongly drive certain brain regions known to be involved in the processing of observed actions using generative adversarial networks – an approach successfully used in the domain of object perception (Murty et al., 2021).

Finally, as described throughout this review, action understanding typically goes hand in hand with planning our own actions, even if the degree to which these two processes mutually depend on each other is still a matter of debate. That said, recent technological developments in virtual reality and mobile human neuroimaging (see e.g. Stangl et al., 2023) enable examining the processes involved in action understanding in the real world and thus open an entirely new approach.

6 Concluding Remarks

Action understanding, like other kinds of understanding, is a complex construct. It covers a broad class of behaviours that are aimed at learning about events in the world, and about the links between cause and effect, including physical and mental causes. Accordingly, a key message of this review is that multiple kinds of cognitive processes and representations are implicated in action understanding, and the nature of these depends on the experience and the goals of the observer.

Many recent treatments of the topic of action understanding begin with the mirror neuron system and work outwards from observations about their properties and ostensibly analogous properties of the human brain and behaviour. This approach has clearly been productive, as witnessed by the resulting explosion of empirical findings and theoretical perspectives. However, it has also sometimes begged the question by assuming a role for mirror neurons and then seeking that role, and in some cases fitting definitions of action understanding around the resulting findings – a form of reverse inference that may be in part responsible for perpetuating controversies around this topic.

In contrast, we have started by asking first why an observer might attend others' actions – what goals this might serve – and then in turn what cognitive and neural machinery might be necessary to achieve those goals. As a guiding framework, we were led by three broad themes: understanding *what* an action is, *how* it is carried out, and *why* it is performed. While these distinctions highlight different requirements of cognitive systems for action understanding, it is also clear that crosstalk amongst these action understanding goals and the implicated systems is probably the norm, rather than the exception, in real-world behaviour.

One point that emerges repeatedly is that predictive processes of various kinds are central to action understanding. These include, for example, abstract predictions that might be made about a hypothetical actor, to guess what kind of action she might carry out given her aims; predictions about the kind of action that is observed, and the intended outcomes, based on the metric details of the actor's grasp and eye movements, objects and the scene (see also Wurm & Schubotz, 2012, 2017); and predictions about the traits of a specific actor, and her future behaviours, based on the evidence of her current actions. Prediction, of course, is arguably central to all forms of perception and of understanding (Kilner et al., 2007). Forming a meaningful model of the world involves the processing of information about what might come next, and also about the possible outcomes of one's own behaviours. In this light, the connection between prediction and action understanding may not be a unique one, but actions, even simple ones, are simply a very rich source of different kinds of cues about the social and physical world.

In sum, we believe that progress in understanding action understanding profits from a focus on diverse kinds of observer goals, and available cues to support those goals. We believe that this approach opens up new avenues for research, especially where paradigms and methods from the domain of object recognition can be transferred to action understanding. We hope that this review inspires the current and next generation of researchers to pick up these threads and to carry out future studies along these lines.

References

Abdollahi, R. O., Jastorff, J., & Orban, G. A. (2013). Common and segregated processing of observed actions in human SPL. *Cerebral Cortex*, *23*(11), 2734–2753.

Adams, R. B., Adams Jr., R. B., Ambady, N., Nakayama, K., & Shimojo, S. (Eds.). (2011). *The Science of Social Vision: The Science of Social Vision* (Vol. 7). Oxford University Press.

Aflalo, T., Zhang, C. Y., Rosario, E. R., et al. (2020). A shared neural substrate for action verbs and observed actions in human posterior parietal cortex. *Science Advances*, *6*(43), 1–16.

Aglioti, S. M., Cesari, P., Romani, M., & Urgesi, C. (2008). Action anticipation and motor resonance in elite basketball players. *Nature Neuroscience*, *11*(9), 1109–1116.

Aksoy, E. E., Orhan, A., & Wörgötter, F. (2017). Semantic decomposition and recognition of long and complex manipulation action sequences. *International Journal of Computer Vision*, *122*(1), 84–115. https://doi.org/10.1007/s11263-016-0956-8.

Ambady, N., & Rosenthal, R. (1992). Thin slices of expressive behavior as predictors of interpersonal consequences: A meta-analysis. *Psychological Bulletin*, *111*(2), 256–274.

Ambrosini, E., Costantini, M., & Sinigaglia, C. (2011). Grasping with the eyes. *Journal of Neurophysiology*, *106*(3), 1437–1442.

Ambrosini, E., Pezzulo, G., & Costantini, M. (2015). The eye in hand: Predicting others' behavior by integrating multiple sources of information. *Journal of Neurophysiology*, *113*(7), 2271–2279.

Amoruso, L., & Finisguerra, A. (2019). Low or high-level motor coding? The role of stimulus complexity. *Frontiers in Human Neuroscience*, *13*, 1–9.

Amoruso, L., & Urgesi, C. (2016). Contextual modulation of motor resonance during the observation of everyday actions. *NeuroImage*, *134*, 74–84.

Anzelotti, S., & Coutanche, M. N. (2018). Beyond functional connectivity: Investigating networks of multivariate representations. *Trends in Cognitive Sciences*, *22*, 258–269.

Anzelotti, S., Caramazza, A., & Saxe, R. (2017). Multivariate pattern dependence. *PloS Computational Biology*, *20*, 1–20. https://doi.org/10.1371/journal.pcbi.1005799.

Arioli, M., & Canessa, N. (2019). Neural processing of social interaction: Coordinate-based meta-analytic evidence from human neuroimaging studies. *Human Brain Mapping, 40*(13), 3712–3737.

Atkinson, A. P., Dittrich, W. H., Gemmell, A. J., & Young, A. W. (2004). Emotion perception from dynamic and static body expressions in point-light and full-light displays. *Perception, 33*(6), 717–746.

Aviezer, H., Trope, Y., & Todorov, A. (2012). Body cues, not facial expressions, discriminate between intense positive and negative emotions. *Science, 338* (6111), 1225–1229.

Axelrod, R. (1980). Effective choice in the prisoner's dilemma. *Journal of Conflict Resolution, 24*(1), 3–25.

Ayzenberg, V., & Behrmann, M. (2022). Does the brain's ventral visual pathway compute object shape? *Trends in Cognitive Sciences*, 1119–1132.

Azaad, S., Knoblich, G., & Sebanz, N. (2021). *Perception and Action in a Social Context*. Cambridge University Press.

Bach, P., & Schenke, K. C. (2017). Predictive social perception: Towards a unifying framework from action observation to person knowledge. *Social and Personality Psychology Compass, 11*(7), 1–17.

Bach, P., Knoblich, G., Gunter, T. C., Friederici, A. D., & Prinz, W. (2005). Action comprehension: Deriving spatial and functional relations. *Journal of Experimental Psychology: Human Perception and Performance, 31*(3), 465–479.

Bach, P., Peatfield, N. A., & Tipper, S. P. (2007). Focusing on body sites: The role of spatial attention in action perception. *Experimental Brain Research, 178*, 509–517.

Bach, P., Nicholson, T., & Hudson, M. (2014). The affordance-matching hypothesis: How objects guide action understanding and prediction. *Frontiers in Human Neuroscience, 8*, 1–13.

Baker, C. L., Saxe, R., & Tenenbaum, J. B. (2009). Action understanding as inverse planning. *Cognition, 113*, 329–349.

Baker, C. L., Jara-Ettinger, J., Saxe, R., & Tenenbaum, J. B. (2017). Rational quantitative attribution of beliefs, desires and percepts in human mentalizing. *Nature Human Behaviour, 1*(4), 1–10.

Baldissera, F., Cavallari, P., Craighero, L., & Fadiga, L. (2001). Modulation of spinal excitability during observation of hand actions in humans. *European Journal of Neuroscience, 13*(1), 190–194.

Bandura, A., & Jeffrey, R. W. (1973). Role of symbolic coding and rehearsal processes in observational learning. *Journal of Personality and Social Psychology, 26*(1), 122–130.

Bandura, A., & Walters, R. H. (1977). *Social Learning Theory* (Vol. 1). Prentice Hall: Englewood cliffs.

Bar, M., Kassam, K. S., Ghuman, A. S., et al. (2006). Top-down facilitation of visual recognition. *Proceedings of the National Academy of Sciences, 103*(2), 449–454.

Bargh, J. A. (1989). Conditional automaticity: Varieties of automatic influence in social perception and cognition. *Unintended Thought*, 3–51.

Baumard, J., & Le Gall, D. (2021). The challenge of apraxia: Toward an operational definition? *Cortex, 141*, 66–80.

Bekkering, H., Wohlschlager, A., & Gattis, M. (2000). Imitation of gestures in children is goal-directed. *The Quarterly Journal of Experimental Psychology: Section A, 53*(1), 153–164.

Benoni, H. (2018). Can automaticity be verified utilizing a perceptual load manipulation? *Psychonomic Bulletin & Review, 25*(6), 2037–2046.

Bestmann, S., & Krakauer, J. W. (2015). The uses and interpretations of the motor-evoked potential for understanding behaviour. *Experimental Brain Research, 233*, 679–689.

Betti, S., Finisguerra, A., Amoruso, L., & Urgesi, C. (2022). Contextual priors guide perception and motor responses to observed actions. *Cerebral Cortex, 32*(3), 608–625.

Beymer, D., & Poggio, T. (1996). Image representations for visual learning. *Science, 272*(5270), 1905–1909.

Binkofski, F., & Buxbaum, L. J. (2013). Two action systems in the human brain. *Brain and Language, 127*(2), 222–229.

Bird, G., Osman, M., Saggerson, A., & Heyes, C. (2005). Sequence learning by action, observation and action observation. *British Journal of Psychology, 96* (3), 371–388.

Blake, R., & Shiffrar, M. (2007). Perception of human motion. *Annual Review of Psychology, 58*, 47–73.

Bonini, L., Rozzi, S., Serventi, F. U., et al. (2010). Ventral premotor and inferior parietal cortices make distinct contribution to action organization and intention understanding. *Cerebral Cortex, 20*, 1372–1385.

Bonini, L., & Ferrari, P. F. (2011). Evolution of mirror systems: a simple mechanism for complex cognitive functions. *Annals of the New York Academy of Sciences, 1225*(1), 166–175.

Bonini, L., Maranesi, M., Livi, A., Fogassi, L., & Rizzolatti, G. (2014). Space-dependent representation of objects' and other's action in monkey ventral premotor grasping neurons. *Journal of Neuroscience, 34*(11), 4108–4119.

Bonini, L., Rotunno, C., Arcuri, E., & Gallese, V. (2022). Mirror neurons 30 years later: Implications and applications. *Trends in Cognitive Sciences*, 767–781.

Bower, G. H., Black, J. B., & Turner, T. J. (1979). Scripts in memory for text. *Cognitive Psychology*, *11*(2), 177–220.

Bowers, J. S., Malhotra, G., Dujmović, M., et al. (2022). Deep problems with neural network models of human vision. *Behavioral and Brain Sciences*, 1–77, 1–74.

Brandman, T., & Peelen, M. V. (2017). Interaction between scene and object processing revealed by human fMRI and MEG decoding. *Journal of Neuroscience*, *37*(32), 7700–7710.

Brass, M., Bekkering, H., Wohlschläger, A., & Prinz, W. (2000). Compatibility between observed and executed finger movements: Comparing symbolic, spatial, and imitative cues. *Brain and Cognition*, *44*(2), 124–143.

Brass, M., Schmitt, R. M., Spengler, S., & Gergely, G. (2007). Investigating action understanding: Inferential processes versus action simulation. *Current Biology*, *17*(24), 2117–2121.

Brincat, S. L., & Connor, C. E. (2004). Underlying principles of visual shape selectivity in posterior inferotemporal cortex. *Nature Neuroscience*, *7*, 880–886.

Buxbaum, L. J., Shapiro, A. D., & Coslett, H. B. (2014). Critical brain regions for tool-related and imitative actions: A componential analysis. *Brain*, *137* (7), 1971–1985.

Cadieu, C. F., Hong, H., Yamins, D. L., et al. (2014). Deep neural networks rival the representation of primate IT cortex for core visual object recognition. *PLoS Computational Biology*, *10*(12), 1–18.

Caggiano, V., Fogassi, L., Rizzolatti, G., Thier, P., & Casile, A. (2009). Mirror neurons differentially encode the peripersonal and extrapersonal space of monkeys. *Science*, *324*(5925), 403–406.

Caggiano, V., Fogassi, L., Rizzolatti, G., et al. (2011). View-based encoding of actions in mirror neurons of area f5 in macaque premotor cortex. *Current Biology*, *21*(2), 144–148.

Caggiano, V., Fogassi, L., Rizzolatti, G., et al. (2012). Mirror neurons encode the subjective value of an observed action. *Proceedings of the National Academy of Sciences*, *109*(29), 11848–11853.

Caggiano, V., Pomper, J. K., Fleischer, F., et al. (2013). Mirror neurons in monkey area F5 do not adapt to the observation of repeated actions. *Nature Communications*, *4*(1), 1–8.

Caggiano, V., Fleischer, F., Pomper, J. K., Giese, M. A., & Thier, P. (2016). Mirror neurons in monkey premotor area F5 show tuning for critical features of visual causality perception. *Current Biology*, *26*(22), 3077–3082.

Calvo-Merino, B., Glaser, D. E., Grèzes, J., Passingham, R. E., & Haggard, P. (2005). Action observation and acquired motor skills: An FMRI study with expert dancers. *Cerebral Cortex*, *15*(8), 1243–1249.

Calvo-Merino, B., Grèzes, J., Glaser, D. E., Passingham, R. E., & Haggard, P. (2006). Seeing or doing? Influence of visual and motor familiarity in action observation. *Current Biology*, *16*(19), 1905–1910.

Camponogara, I., Rodger, M., Craig, C., & Cesari, P. (2017). Expert players accurately detect an opponent's movement intentions through sound alone. *Journal of Experimental Psychology: Human Perception and Performance*, *43*(2), 348–359.

Cappa, S. F., Binetti, G., Pezzini, A., et al. (1998). Object and action naming in Alzheimer's disease and frontotemporal dementia. *Neurology*, *50*(2), 351–355.

Caramazza, A., Anzellotti, S., Strnad, L., & Lingnau, A. (2014). Embodied cognition and mirror neurons: A critical assessment. *Annual Review of Neuroscience*, *37*, 1–15.

Casile, A., & Giese, M. A. (2006). Nonvisual motor training influences biological motion perception. *Current Biology*, *16*(1), 69–74.

Caspers, S., Zilles, K., Laird, A. R., & Eickhoff, S. B. (2010). ALE meta-analysis of action observation and imitation in the human brain. *Neuroimage*, *50*(3), 1148–1167.

Catmur, C. (2016). Automatic imitation? Imitative compatibility affects responses at high perceptual load. *Journal of Experimental Psychology: Human Perception and Performance*, *42*(4), 530–539.

Catmur, C., Walsh, V., & Heyes, C. (2007). Sensorimotor learning configures the human mirror system. *Current Biology*, *17*(17), 1527–1531.

Cattaneo, L., Sandrini, M., & Schwarzbach, J. (2010). State-dependent TMS reveals a hierarchical representation of observed acts in the temporal, parietal and premotor cortices. *Cerebral Cortex*, *20*(9), 2252–2258.

Cavallo, A., Koul, A., Ansuini, C., Capozzi, F., & Becchio, C. (2016). Decoding intentions from movement kinematics. *Scientific Reports*, *6*(1), 1–8.

Cavanagh, P., Caplovitz, G. P., Lytchenko, T. K., Maechler, M. R., Tse, P. U., & Sheinberg, D. L. (2023). The Architecture of Object-Based Attention. *Psychonomic Bulletin & Review*, 1–25.

Cerliani, L., Bhandari, R., De Angelis, L., et al. (2022). Predictive coding during action observation – A depth-resolved intersubject functional correlation study at 7T. *Cortex*, *148*, 121–138.

Chartrand, T. L., & Bargh, J. A. (1999). The chameleon effect: The perception–behavior link and social interaction. *Journal of Personality and Social Psychology*, *76*(6), 893–910.

Chersi, F., Ferrari, P. F., & Fogassi, L. (2011). Neuronal chains for actions in the parietal lobe: A computational model. *PloS one*, *6*(11), 1–15.

Chong, T. T. J., Cunnington, R., Williams, M. A., Kanwisher, N., & Mattingley, J. B. (2008). fMRI adaptation reveals mirror neurons in human inferior parietal cortex. *Current Biology*, *18*(20), 1576–1580.

Chong, T. T. J., Cunnington, R., Williams, M. A., & Mattingley, J. B. (2009). The role of selective attention in matching observed and executed actions. *Neuropsychologia*, *47*(3), 786–795.

Christensen, J. F., & Calvo-Merino, B. (2013). Dance as a subject for empirical aesthetics. *Psychology of Aesthetics, Creativity, and the Arts*, *7*(1), 76–88.

Chun, M. M., Golomb, J. D., & Turk-Browne, N. B. (2011). A taxonomy of external and internal attention. *Annual Review of Psychology*, *62*(1), 73–101.

Cichy, R. M., & Kaiser, D. (2019). Deep neural networks as scientific models. *Trends in Cognitive Sciences*, *23*, 305–317.

Cisek, P. (2007). Cortical mechanisms of action selection: The affordance competition hypothesis. *Philosophical Transactions of the Royal Society B: Biological Sciences*, *362*(1485), 1585–1599.

Cisek, P. (2019). Resynthesizing behavior through phylogenetic refinement. *Attention, Perception, & Psychophysics*, *81*, 2265–2287.

Collins, A. M., & Quillian, M. R. (1969). Retrieval time from semantic memory. *Journal of Verbal Learning and Verbal Behavior*, *8*(2), 240–247.

Cook, R., Bird, G., Catmur, C., Press, C., & Heyes, C. (2014). Mirror neurons: From origin to function. *Behavioral and Brain Sciences*, *37*(2), 177–192.

Cracco, E., Bardi, L., Desmet, C., et al. (2018). Automatic imitation: A meta-analysis. *Psychological Bulletin*, *144*(5), 453–500.

Cross, E. S., Hamilton, A. F. D. C., & Grafton, S. T. (2006). Building a motor simulation de novo: Observation of dance by dancers. *Neuroimage*, *31*(3), 1257–1267.

Csibra, G. (2008). Action mirroring and action understanding: An alternative account. *Sensorimotor Foundations of Higher Cognition: Attention and Performance XXII*, 435–459.

Cusack, J. P., Williams, J. H., & Neri, P. (2015). Action perception is intact in autism spectrum disorder. *Journal of Neuroscience*, *35*(5), 1849–1857.

Darda, K. M., & Ramsey, R. (2019). The inhibition of automatic imitation: A meta-analysis and synthesis of fMRI studies. *NeuroImage*, *197*, 320–329.

de la Rosa, S., Schillinger, F. L., Bülthoff, H. H., Schultz, J., & Umildag, K. (2016). fMRI adaptation between action observation and action execution reveals cortical areas with mirror neuron properties in human BA 44/45. *Frontiers in Human Neuroscience*, 1–11. https://doi.org/10.3389/fnhum.2016.00078.

de Lange, F. P., Spronk, M., Willems, R. M., Toni, I., & Bekkering, H. (2008). Complementary systems for understanding action intentions. *Current Biology, 18*(6), 454–457.

de Lange, F. P., Heilbron, M., & Kok, P. (2018). How do expectations shape perception? *Trends in Cognitive Sciences, 22*(9), 764–779.

Dennett, D. C. (1987). *The Intentional Stance*. MIT press.

Di Pellegrino, G., Fadiga, L., Fogassi, L., Gallese, V., & Rizzolatti, G. (1992). Understanding motor events: A neurophysiological study. *Experimental Brain Research, 91*, 176–180.

Dima, D. C., Tomita, T. M., Honey, C. J., & Isik, L. (2022). Social-affective features drive human representations of observed actions. *Elife, 11*, 1–22.

Dinstein, I., Hasson, U., Rubin, N., & Heeger, D. J. (2007). Brain areas selective for both observed and executed movements. *Journal of Neurophysiology, 98*(3), 1415–1427.

Dinstein, I., Thomas, C., Behrmann, M., & Heeger, D. J. (2008). A mirror up to nature. *Current Biology, 18*(1), R13–R18.

Donnarumma, F., Costantini, M., Ambrosini, E., Friston, K., & Pezzulo, G. (2017). Action perception as hypothesis testing. *Cortex, 89*, 45–60.

Dungan, J. A., Stepanovic, M., & Young, L. (2016). Theory of mind for processing unexpected events across contexts. *Social Cognitive and Affective Neuroscience, 11*(8), 1183–1192.

Edelman, S. (1998). Representation is representation of similarities. *Behavioral and Brain Sciences, 21*, 449–498.

Epstein, R. A., & Baker, C. I. (2019). Scene perception in the human brain. *Annual Review of Vision Science, 5*, 373–397.

Ernst, M. O. (2006). A Bayesian view on multimodal integration Cue. *Human Body Perception from the Inside Out*, 105–131.

Estes, S. G. (1938). Judging personality from expressive behavior. *The Journal of Abnormal and Social Psychology, 33*(2), 217–236.

Fadiga, L., Fogassi, L., Pavesi, G., & Rizzolatti, G. (1995). Motor facilitation during action observation: A magnetic stimulation study. *Journal of Neurophysiology, 73*(6), 2608–2611.

Ferrari, P. F., Bonini, L., & Fogassi, L. (2009). From monkey mirror neurons to primate behaviours: Possible 'direct' and 'indirect' pathways. *Philosophical Transactions of the Royal Society B: Biological Sciences, 364*(1528), 2311–2323.

Finisguerra, A., Amoruso, L., Makris, S., & Urgesi, C. (2018). Dissociated representations of deceptive intentions and kinematic adaptations in the observer's motor system. *Cerebral Cortex, 28*(1), 33–47.

Flanagan, J. R., & Johansson, R. S. (2003). Action plans used in action observation. *Nature*, *424*(6950), 769–771.

Fleischer, F., Caggiano, V., Thier, P., & Giese, M. A. (2013). Physiologically inspired model for the visual recognition of transitive hand actions. *Journal of Neuroscience*, *33*, 6563–6580.

Fogassi, L., Ferrari, P. F., Gesierich, B., et al. (2005). Parietal lobe: From action organization to intention understanding. *Science*, *308*(5722), 662–667.

Frith, C. D., & Done, D. J. (1988). Towards a neuropsychology of schizophrenia. *The British Journal of Psychiatry*, *153*(4), 437–443.

Gallese, V., Fadiga, L., Fogassi, L., & Rizzolatti, G. (1996). Action recognition in the premotor cortex. *Brain*, *119*(2), 593–609.

Gangitano, M., Mottaghy, F. M., & Pascual-Leone, A. (2001). Phase-specific modulation of cortical motor output during movement observation. *Neuroreport*, *12*, 1489–1492.

Gangitano, M., Mottaghy, F. M., & Pascual-Leone, A. (2004). Modulation of premotor mirror neuron activity during observation of unpredictable grasping movements. *European Journal of Neuroscience*, *20*(8), 2193–2202.

Gärdenfors, P. (2004). *Conceptual Spaces: The Geometry of Thought*. MIT press.

Gardner, T., Aglinskas, A., & Cross, E. S. (2017). Using guitar learning to probe the action observation network's response to visuomotor familiarity. *NeuroImage*, *156*, 174–189.

Georgopoulos, A. P. (1990). Neurophysiology of reaching. In M. Jeannerod (Ed.), *Attention and performance 13: Motor representation and control* (pp. 227–263). Lawrence Erlbaum Associates, Inc.

Gibson, J. J. (1979/2014). *The Ecological Approach to Visual Perception: Classic Edition*. Psychology Press.

Giese, M. A., & Poggio, T. (2003). Neural mechanisms for the recognition of biological movements. *Nature Reviews Neuroscience*, *4*(3), 179–192.

Gilbert, D. T., & Malone, P. S. (1995). The correspondence bias. *Psychological Bulletin*, *117*(1), 21–38.

Gilboa, A., & Marlatte, H. (2017). Neurobiology of schemas and schema-mediated memory. *Trends in Cognitive Sciences*, *21*, 618–631.

Goodale, M. A., & Milner, A. D. (1992). Separate visual pathways for perception and action. *Trends in Neurosciences*, *15*(1), 20–25.

Grafton, S. T., Arbib, M. A., Fadiga, L., & Rizzolatti, G. (1996). Localization of grasp representations in humans by positron emission tomography: 2. Observation compared with imagination. *Experimental Brain Research*, *112*, 103–111.

Green, C., & Hummel, J. E. (2006). Familiar interacting object pairs are perceptually grouped. *Journal of Experimental Psychology: Human Perception and Performance, 32*(5), 1107–1119.

Grill-Spector, K., & Malach, R. (2001). fMR-adaptation: A tool for studying the functional properties of human cortical neurons. *Acta Psychologica, 107*(1–3), 293–321.

Güçlü, U., & van Gerven, M. A. J. (2015). Deep neural networks reveal a gradient in the complexity of neural representations across the ventral stream. *Journal of Neuroscience, 35*, 10005–10014.

Hafri, A., & Firestone, C. (2021). The perception of relations. *Trends in Cognitive Sciences, 25*(6), 475–492.

Hafri, A., Trueswell, J. C., & Epstein, R. A. (2017). Neural representations of observed actions generalize across static and dynamic visual input. *Journal of Neuroscience, 37*(11), 3056–3071.

Hamilton, A. F., & Grafton, S. T. (2007). The motor hierarchy: From kinematics to goals and intentions. *Sensorimotor Foundations of Higher Cognition, 22*, 381–408.

Hamilton, A. F., & Grafton, S. T. (2008). Action outcomes are represented in human inferior frontoparietal cortex. *Cerebral Cortex, 18*(5), 1160–1168.

Hamilton, A. F. D. C., & Grafton, S. T. (2006). Goal representation in human anterior intraparietal sulcus. *Journal of Neuroscience, 26*(4), 1133–1137.

Hardwick, R. M., Caspers, S., Eickhoff, S. B., & Swinnen, S. P. (2018). Neural correlates of action: Comparing meta-analyses of imagery, observation, and execution. *Neuroscience and Biobehavioral Reviews, 94*, 31–44.

Hari, R. (2006). Action–perception connection and the cortical mu rhythm. *Progress in Brain Research, 159*, 253–260.

Harpaz, N. K., Flash, T., & Dinstein, I. (2014). Scale-invariant movement encoding in the human motor system. *Neuron, 81*(2), 452–462.

Hemed, E., Mark-Tavger, I., Hertz, U., Bakbani-Elkayam, S., & Eitam, B. (2021). Automatically controlled: Task irrelevance fully cancels otherwise automatic imitation. *Journal of Experimental Psychology: General*, 996–1017.

Heyes, C. (2001). Causes and consequences of imitation. *Trends in Cognitive Sciences, 5*(6), 253–261.

Heyes, C., & Catmur, C. (2022). What happened to mirror neurons? *Perspectives on Psychological Science, 17*(1), 153–168.

Hickok, G. (2009). Eight problems for the mirror neuron theory of action understanding in monkeys and humans. *Journal of Cognitive Neuroscience, 21*(7), 1229–1243.

Hobson, H. M., & Bishop, D. V. (2017). The interpretation of mu suppression as an index of mirror neuron activity: Past, present and future. *Royal Society Open Science*, *4*(3), 1–22.

Hutchinson, J. B., & Barrett, L. F. (2019). The power of predictions: An emerging paradigm for psychological research. *Current Directions in Psychological Science*, *28*(3), 280–291.

Iacoboni, M. (2009). Imitation, empathy, and mirror neurons. *Annual Review of Psychology*, *60*, 653–670.

Iacoboni, M., Woods, R. P., Brass, M., et al. (1999). Cortical mechanisms of human imitation. *Science*, *286*(5449), 2526–2528.

Jellema, T., Baker, C. I., Wicker, B., & Perrett, D. I. (2000). Neural representation for the perception of the intentionality of actions. *Brain and Cognition*, *44*, 280–302.

Johnson, K. L., Gill, S., Reichman, V., & Tassinary, L. G. (2007). Swagger, sway, and sexuality: Judging sexual orientation from body motion and morphology. *Journal of Personality and Social Psychology*, *93*(3), 321–334.

Jola, C., Abedian-Amiri, A., Kuppuswamy, A., Pollick, F. E., & Grosbras, M. H. (2012). Motor simulation without motor expertise: Enhanced corticospinal excitability in visually experienced dance spectators. *PloS one*, *7*(3), 1–2.

Kabulska, Z., & Lingnau, A. (2022). The cognitive structure underlying the organization of observed actions. *Behavior Research Methods*, *55*, 1890–1906.

Kaiser, D., Quek, G. L., Cichy, R. M., & Peelen, M. V. (2019). Object vision in a structured world. *Trends in Cognitive Sciences*, *23*(8), 672–685.

Kalénine, S., Buxbaum, L. J., & Coslett, H. B. (2010). Critical brain regions for action recognition: Lesion symptom mapping in left hemisphere stroke. *Brain*, *133*(11), 3269–3280.

Kelly, S. W., Burton, A. M., Riedel, B., & Lynch, E. (2003). Sequence learning by action and observation: Evidence for separate mechanisms. *British Journal of Psychology*, *94*(3), 355–372.

Kemmerer, D. (2021). What modulates the Mirror Neuron System during action observation? Multiple factors involving the action, the actor, the observer, the relationship between actor and observer, and the context. *Progress in Biology*, *205*, 1–24.

Kemp, C., & Tenenbaum, J. B. (2008). The discovery of structural form. *Proceedings of the National Academy of Sciences*, *105*(31), 10687–10692.

Kilner, J. M. (2011). More than one pathway to action understanding. *Trends in Cognitive Sciences*, *15*(8), 352–357.

Kilner, J. M., Friston, K. J., & Frith, C. D. (2007). Predictive coding: An account of the mirror neuron system. *Cognitive Processing*, *8*, 159–166.

Kilner, J. M., Kraskov, A., & Lemon, R. N. (2014). Do monkey F5 mirror neurons show changes in firing rate during repeated observation of natural actions? *Journal of Neurophysiology, 111*(6), 1214–1226.

Kilner, J. M., & Lemon, R. N. (2013). What we know currently about mirror neurons. *Current Biology, 23*(23), R1057–R1062.

Kilner, J. M., Vargas, C., Duval, S., Blakemore, S. J., Sirigu, A. (2004). Motor activation prior to observation of a predicted movement. *Nature Neuroscience, 7*(12), 1299–1301.

Kilner, J. M., Neal, A., Weiskopf, N., Friston, K. J., & Frith, C. D. (2009). Evidence of mirror neurons in human inferior frontal gyrus. *Journal of Neuroscience, 29*(32), 10153–10159.

Knoblich, G., & Flach, R. (2001). Predicting the effects of actions: Interactions of perception and action. *Psychological Science, 12*, 467–472.

Kohler, E., Keysers, C., Umilta, M. A., et al. (2002). Hearing sounds, understanding actions: Action representation in mirror neurons. *Science, 297* (5582), 846–848.

Kozlowski, L. T., & Cutting, J. E. (1977). Recognizing the sex of a walker from a dynamic point-light display. *Perception & Psychophysics, 21*, 575–580.

Kramer, R. S., Arend, I., & Ward, R. (2010). Perceived health from biological motion predicts voting behaviour. *The Quarterly Journal of Experimental Psychology, 63*(4), 625–632.

Kraskov, A., Dancause, N., Quallo, M. M., Shepert, S., & Lemon, R. N. (2009). Corticospinal neurons in macaque ventral premotor cortex with mirror properties: A potential mechanism for action suppression? *Neuron, 64*, 922–930.

Kravitz, D. J., Saleem, K. S., Baker, C. I., Ungerleider, L. G., & Mishkin, M. (2013). The ventral visual pathway: An expanded neural framework for the processing of object quality. *Trends in Cognitive Sciences, 17*(1), 26–49.

Kriegeskorte, N., & Kievit, R. A. (2013). Representational geometry: Integrating cognition, computation, and the brain. *Trends in Cognitive Sciences, 17*(8), 401–412.

Kriegeskorte, N., & Mur, M. (2012). Inverse MDS: Inferring dissimilarity structure from multiple item arrangements. *Frontiers in Psychology, 3*, 1–13.

Kriegeskorte, N., Goebel, R., & Bandettini, P. (2006). Information-based functional brain mapping. *Proceedings of the National Academy of Sciences, 103* (10), 3863–3868.

Kriegeskorte, N., Mur, M., & Bandettini, P. (2008a). Representational similarity analysis – connecting the branches of systems neuroscience. *Frontiers in Systems Neuroscience, 2*, 1–28.

Kriegeskorte, N., Mur, M., Ruff, D. A., et al. (2008b). Matching categorical object representations in inferior temporal cortex of man and monkey. *Neuron*, *60*(6), 1126–1141.

Kroczek, L. O., Lingnau, A., Schwind, V., Wolff, C., & Mühlberger, A. (2021). Angry facial expressions bias towards aversive actions. *Plos one*, *16*(9), 1–13.

Lanzilotto, M., Maranesi, M., Livi, A., et al. (2020). Stable readout of observed actions from format-dependent activity of monkey's anterior intraparietal neurons. *Proceedings of the National Academy of Sciences*, *117*(28), 16596–16605.

Lavie, N., & Dalton, P. (2014). Load theory of attention and cognitive control. *The Oxford Handbook of Attention*, 56–75.

Levin, B. (1993). *English Verb Classes and Alternations*. Chicago: The University of Chicago Press.

Lingnau, A., & Downing, P. E. (2015). The lateral occipitotemporal cortex in action. *Trends in Cognitive Sciences*, *19*(5), 268–277.

Lingnau, A., & Petris, S. (2013). Action understanding inside and outside the motor system: The role of task difficulty. *Cerebral Cortex*, *23*(6), 1342–1350. https://doi.org/10.1093/cercor/bhs112.

Lingnau, A., Gesierich, B., & Caramazza, A. (2009). Asymmetric fMRI adaptation reveals no evidence for mirror neurons in humans. *Proceedings of the National Academy of Sciences*, *106*(24), 9925–9930.

Liu, S., Brooks, N. B., & Spelke, E. S. (2019). Origins of the concepts cause, cost, and goal in prereaching infants. *Proceedings of the National Academy of Sciences*, *116*(36), 17747–17752.

Livi, A., Lanzilotto, M., Maranesi, M., et al. (2019). Agent-based representations of objects and actions in the monkey pre-supplementary motor area. *Proceedings of the National Academy of Sciences*, *116*(7), 2691–2700.

Loula, F., Prasad, S., Harber, K., & Shiffrar, M. (2005). Recognizing people from their movement. *Journal of Experimental Psychology: Human Perception and Performance*, *31*(1), 210–220.

Maeda, F., Kleiner-Fisman, G., & Pascual-Leone, A. (2002). Motor facilitation while observing hand actions: Specificity of the effect and role of observer's orientation. *Journal of Neurophysiology*, *87*(3), 1329–1335.

Majdandžić, J., Bekkering, H., van Schie, H. T., & Toni, I. (2009). Movement-specific repetition suppression in ventral and dorsal premotor cortex during action observation. *Cerebral Cortex*, *19*(11), 2736–2745.

Maranesi, M., Livi, A., & Bonini, L. (2017). Spatial and viewpoint selectivity for others' observed actions in monkey ventral premotor mirror neurons. *Scientific Reports*, *7*(1), 1–7.

Marr, D, (1982). *Vision*. W.H. Freeman.

Mattar, A. A., & Gribble, P. L. (2005). Motor learning by observing. *Neuron, 46* (1), 153–160.

McDonough, K. L., Hudson, M., & Bach, P. (2019). Cues to intention bias action perception toward the most efficient trajectory. *Scientific Reports, 9* (1), 1–10.

McMahon, E., & Isik, L. (2023). Seeing social interactions. *Trends in Cognitive Science, 27*(12), 1165–1179.

Meltzoff, A. N., & Moore, M. K. (1977). Imitation of facial and manual gestures by human neonates. *Science, 198*(4312), 75–78.

Milner, A. D., & Goodale, M. A. (1995). *The Visual Brain in Action*. Oxford: Oxford University Press.

Minsky, M. (1975). Minsky's Frame System Theory. Proceedings of the 1975 workshop on theoretical issues in natural language processing, pages 104–116.

Morris, M. W., & Murphy, G. L. (1990). Converging operations on a basic level in event taxonomies. *Memory & Cognition, 18*(4), 407–418.

Muhammad, K., Ullah, A., Imran, A. S., et al. (2021). Human action recognition using attention based LSTM network with dilated CNN features. *Future Generation Computer Systems, 125*, 820–830.

Mukamel, R., Ekstrom, A. D., Kaplan, J., Iacoboni, M., & Fried, I. (2010). Single-neuron responses in humans during execution and observation of actions. *Current Biology, 20*(8), 750–756.

Muthukumaraswamy, S. D., & Johnson, B. W. (2004a). Changes in rolandic mu rhythm during observation of a precision grip. *Psychophysiology, 41*(1), 152–156.

Muthukumaraswamy, S. D., Johnson, B. W., & McNair, N. A. (2004b). Mu rhythm modulation during observation of an object-directed grasp. *Cognitive Brain Research, 19*(2), 195–201.

Murata, A., Fadiga, L., Fogassi, L., et al. (1997). Object representation in the ventral premotor cortex (area F5) of the monkey. *Journal of Neurophysiology, 78*(4), 2226–2230.

Murty, N. A. R., Bashivan, P., Abate, A., DiCarlo, J. J., & Kanwisher, N. (2021). Computational models of category-selective brain regions enable high-throughput tests of selectivity. *Nature Communications, 12*, 1–14.

Nastase, S. A., Connolly, A. C., Oosterhof, N. N., et al. (2017). Attention selectively reshapes the geometry of distributed semantic representation. *Cerebral Cortex, 27*(8), 4277–4291.

Netanyahu, A., Shu, T., Katz, B., Barbu, A., & Tenenbaum, J. B. (2021). Phase: Physically-grounded abstract social events for machine social perception. In

Proceedings of the aaai Conference on Artificial Intelligence, 35(1), 845–853.

Norman, K. A., Polyn, S. M., Detre, G. J., & Haxby, J. V. (2006). Beyond mind-reading: Multi-voxel pattern analysis of fMRI data. *Trends in Cognitive Sciences, 10*(9), 424–430.

Nosofsky, R. M. (1986). Attention, similarity, and the identification–categorization relationship. *Journal of Experimental Psychology: General, 115*(1), 39–57.

Oliva, A., & Torralba, A. (2007). The role of context in object recognition. *Trends in Cognitive Sciences, 11*(12), 520–527.

Oostenbroek, J., Suddendorf, T., Nielsen, M., et al. (2016). Comprehensive longitudinal study challenges the existence of neonatal imitation in humans. *Current Biology, 26*, 1334–1338.

Oosterhof, N. N., Wiggett, A. J., Diedrichsen, J., Tipper, S. P., & Downing, P. E. (2010). Surface-based information mapping reveals crossmodal vision–action representations in human parietal and occipitotemporal cortex. *Journal of Neurophysiology, 104*(2), 1077–1089.

Oosterhof, N. N., Tipper, S. P., & Downing, P. E. (2012a). Viewpoint (in)dependence of action representations: An MVPA study. *Journal of Cognitive Neuroscience, 24*(4), 975–989.

Oosterhof, N. N., Tipper, S. P., & Downing, P. E. (2012b). Visuo-motor imagery of specific manual actions: A multi-variate pattern analysis fMRI study. *Neuroimage, 63*(1), 262–271.

Oosterhof, N. N., Tipper, S. P., & Downing, P. E. (2013). Crossmodal and action-specific: Neuroimaging the human mirror neuron system. *Trends in Cognitive Sciences, 17*(7), 311–318.

Orban, G. A., Ferri, S., & Platonov, A. (2019). The role of putative human anterior intraparietal sulcus area in observed manipulative action discrimination. *Brain and Behavior, 9*, 1–13.

Orban, G. A., Lanzilotto, M., & Bonini, L. (2021). From observed action identity to social affordances. *Trends in Cognitive Sciences, 25*(6), 493–505.

Orgs, G., Hagura, N., & Haggard, P. (2013). Learning to like it: Aesthetic perception of bodies, movements and choreographic structure. *Consciousness and Cognition, 22*(2), 603–612.

Osiurak, F., & Badets, A. (2016). Tool use and affordance: Manipulation-based versus reasoning-based approaches. *Psychological Review, 123*(5), 534–568.

Oztop, E., Wolpert, D., & Kawato, M. (2005). Mental state inference using visual control parameters. *Cognitive Brain Research, 22*, 129–151.

Oztop, E., Kawato, M., & Arbib, M. A. (2013). Mirror neurons: Functions, mechanisms, and models. *Neuroscience Letters, 540*, 43–55.

Papeo, L. (2020). Twos in human visual perception. *Cortex*, *132*, 473–478.

Papeo, L., Agostini, B., & Lingnau, A. (2019). The large-scale organization of gestures and words in the middle temporal gyrus. *Journal of Neuroscience*, *39*(30), 5966–5974.

Peelen, M. V., & Downing, P. E. (2007). Using multi-voxel pattern analysis of fMRI data to interpret overlapping functional activations. *Trends in Cognitive Sciences*, *11*(1), 4–4.

Peelen, M. V., & Kastner, S. (2014). Attention in the real world: Toward understanding its neural basis. *Trends in Cognitive Sciences*, *18*(5), 242–250.

Perrett, D. I., Harries, M. H., Bevan, R., et al. (1989). Frameworks of analysis for the neural representation of animate objects and actions. *Journal of Experimental Biology*, *146*(1), 87–113.

Petrini, K., Pollick, F. E., Dahl, S., et al. (2011). Action expertise reduces brain activity for audiovisual matching actions: An fMRI study with expert drummers. *Neuroimage*, *56*(3), 1480–1492.

Pinker, S. L. (1989). *Cognition: The Acquisition of Argument Structure*. MIT Press.

Pitcher, D., & Ungerleider, L. G. (2021). Evidence for a third visual pathway specialized for social perception. *Trends in Cognitive Sciences*, *25*(2), 100–110.

Poldrack, R. A. (2006). Can cognitive processes be inferred from neuroimaging data? *Trends in Cognitive Sciences*, *10*(2), 59–63.

Press, C., Weiskopf, N., & Kilner, J. M. (2012). Dissociable roles of human inferior frontal gyrus during action execution and observation. *Neuroimage*, *60*(3), 1671–1677.

Prinz, W. (1997). Perception and action planning. *European Journal of Cognitive Psychology*, *9*(2), 129–154.

Quadflieg, S., & Westmoreland, K. (2019). Making sense of other people's encounters: Towards an integrative model of relational impression formation. *Journal of Nonverbal Behavior*, *43*, 233–256.

Ramsey, R., Darda, K. M., & Downing, P. E. (2019). Automatic imitation remains unaffected under cognitive load. *Journal of Experimental Psychology: Human Perception and Performance*, *45*(5), 601–615.

Rao, R. P., & Ballard, D. H. (1999). Predictive coding in the visual cortex: A functional interpretation of some extra-classical receptive-field effects. *Nature Neuroscience*, *2*(1), 79–87.

Reddy, V., & Uithol, S. (2016). Engagement: Looking beyond the mirror to understand action understanding. *British Journal of Developmental Psychology*, *34*, 101–114.

Repp, B. H., & Knoblich, G. (2004). Perceiving action identity: How pianists recognize their own performances. *Psychological Science, 15*(9), 604–609.

Rifkin, A. (1985). Evidence for a basic level in event taxonomies. *Memory & Cognition, 13*(6), 538–556.

Riley, M. R., & Constantinidis, C. (2016). Role of prefrontal persistent activity in working memory. *Frontiers in Systems Neuroscience, 9*, 1–14.

Rizzolatti, G., & Craighero, L. (2004). The mirror-neuron system. *Annual Review of Neuroscience, 27*, 169–192.

Rizzolatti, G., & Fogassi, L. (2014). The mirror mechanism: Recent findings and perspectives. *Philosophical Transactions of the Royal Society B: Biological Sciences, 369*(1644), 1–12.

Rizzolatti, G., & Sinigaglia, C. (2010). The functional role of the parieto-frontal mirror circuit: Interpretations and misinterpretations. *Nature Reviews Neuroscience, 11*(4), 264–274.

Rizzolatti, G., & Sinigaglia, C. (2016). The mirror mechanism: A basic principle of brain function. *Nature Reviews Neuroscience, 17*(12), 757–765.

Rizzolatti, G., Scandolara, C., Gentilucci, M., & Camarda, R. (1981). Response properties and behavioral modulation of 'mouth' neurons of the postarcuate cortex (area 6) in macaque monkeys. *Brain Research, 225*(2), 421–424.

Rizzolatti, G., Camarda, R., Fogassi, L., et al. (1988). Functional organization of inferior area 6 in the macaque monkey: II. Area F5 and the control of distal movements. *Experimental Brain Research, 71*, 491–507.

Rizzolatti, G., Fadiga, L., Matelli, M., et al. (1996). Localization of grasp representations in humans by PET: 1. Observation versus execution. *Experimental Brain Research, 111*, 246–252.

Rizzolatti, G., Fogassi, L., & Gallese, V. (2001). Neurophysiological mechanisms underlying the understanding and imitation of action. *Nature Reviews Neuroscience, 2*(9), 661–670.

Rosch, E., Mervis, C. B., Gray, W. D., Johnson, D. M., & Boyes-Braem, P. (1976). Basic objects in natural categories. *Cognitive Psychology, 8*(3), 382–439.

Ross, L. (2018). From the fundamental attribution error to the truly fundamental attribution error and beyond: My research journey. *Perspectives on Psychological Science, 13*(6), 750–769.

Saxe, R., & Kanwisher, N. (2003). People thinking about thinking people: The role of the temporo-parietal junction in 'theory of mind'. *Neuroimage, 19*(4), 1835–1842.

Schank, R. C., & Abelson, R. P. (1977). *Scripts, Plans, Goals, and Understanding: An Inquiry into Human Knowledge Structures.* Psychology press.

Schultz, J., & Frith, C. D. (2022). Animacy and the prediction of behaviour. *Neuroscience & Biobehavioral Reviews*, *140*, 1–11.

Schurz, M., Radua, J., Aichhorn, M., Richlan, F., & Perner, J. (2014). Fractionating theory of mind: A meta-analysis of functional brain imaging studies. *Neuroscience & Biobehavioral Reviews*, *42*, 9–34.

Sebanz, N., & Knoblich, G. (2021). Progress in joint-action research. *Current Directions in Psychological Science*, *30*(2), 138–143.

Seeliger, K., Ambrogioni, L., Güçlütürk, Y., et al. (2021). End-to-end neural system identification with neural information flow. *PLoS Computational Biology*, *17*(2), 1–22.

Seger, C. A. (1997). Two forms of sequential implicit learning. *Consciousness and Cognition*, *6*(1), 108–131.

Serences, J. T., Schwarzbach, J., Courtney, S. M., Golay, X., & Yantis, S. (2004). Control of object-based attention in human cortex. *Cerebral Cortex*, *14*(12), 1346–1357.

Shahdloo, M., Çelik, E., Urgen, B. A., Gallant, J. L., & Çukur, T. (2022). Task-dependent warping of semantic representations during search for visual action categories. *Journal of Neuroscience*, *42*(35), 6782–6799.

Shepard, R. N. (1958). Stimulus and response generalization: Tests of a model relating generalization to distance in psychological space. *Journal of Experimental Psychology*, *55*(6), 509–523.

Singer, J. M., & Sheinberg, D. L. (2010). Temporal cortex neurons encode articulated actions as slow sequences of integrated poses. *Journal of Neuroscience*, *30*(8), 3133–3145.

Sliwa, J., & Freiwald, W. A. (2017). A dedicated network for social interaction processing in the primate brain. *Science*, *356*, 745–749.

Southgate, V. (2013). Do infants provide evidence that the mirror system is involved in action understanding? *Consciousness and Cognition*, *22*(3), 1114–1121.

Spoerer, C. J., McClure, P., & Kriegeskorte, N. (2017). Recurrent convolutional neural networks: A better model of biological object recognition. *Frontiers in Psychology*, *8*, 1–14.

Spunt, R. P., & Lieberman, M. D. (2013). The busy social brain: Evidence for automaticity and control in the neural systems supporting social cognition and action understanding. *Psychological Science*, *24*(1), 80–86.

Spunt, R. P., & Lieberman, M. D. (2014). Automaticity, control, and the social brain. In J. W. Sherman, B. Gawronski, & Y. Trope (Eds.), *Dual-process theories of the social mind* (pp. 279–298). New York, NY: Guilford Press.

Spunt, R. P., Satpute, A. B., & Lieberman, M. D. (2011). Identifying the what, why, and how of an observed action: An fMRI study of mentalizing and mechanizing during action observation. *Journal of Cognitive Neuroscience*, *23*(1), 63–74.

Spunt, R. P., Kemmerer, D., & Adolphs, R. (2016). The neural basis of conceptualizing the same action at different levels of abstraction. *Social Cognitive and Affective Neuroscience*, *11*(7), 1141–1151.

Stangl, M., Maoz, S. L., & Suthana, N. (2023). Mobile cognition: Imaging the brain in the 'real world'. *Nature Reviews Neuroscience*, *24*, 347–362.

Strafella, A. P., & Paus, T. (2000). Modulation of cortical excitability during action observation: A transcranial magnetic stimulation study. *Neuroreport*, *11*(10), 2289–2292.

Summerfield, C., Trittschuh, E. H., Monti, J. M., Mesulam, M. M., & Egner, T. (2008). Neural repetition suppression reflects fulfilled perceptual expectations. *Nature Neuroscience*, *11*(9), 1004–1006.

Talmy, L. (1985). Lexicalization patterns: Semantic structure in lexical forms. *Language Typology and Syntactic Description*, *3*(99), 36–149.

Tamir, D. I., & Thornton, M. A. (2018). Modeling the predictive social mind. *Trends in Cognitive Sciences*, *22*(3), 201–212.

Tanaka, K. (1997). Mechanisms of visual object recognition: Monkey and human studies. *Current Opinion in Neurobiology*, *7*, 523–529.

Tarhan, L., & Konkle, T. (2020). Sociality and interaction envelope organize visual action representations. *Nature Communications*, *11*(1), 1–11.

Tarhan, L., de Freitas, J., & Konkle, T. (2021). Behavioral and neural representations en route to intuitive action understanding. *Neuropsychologia*, *163*, 1–10.

Thompson, E. L., Bird, G., & Catmur, C. (2019). Conceptualizing and testing action understanding. *Neuroscience & Biobehavioral Reviews*, *105*, 106–114.

Thompson, E. L., Long, E. L., Bird, G., & Catmur, C. (2023). Is action understanding an automatic process? Both cognitive and perceptual processing are required for the identification of actions and intentions. *Quarterly Journal of Experimental Psychology*, *76*(1), 70–83.

Thompson, J., & Parasuraman, R. (2012). Attention, biological motion, and action recognition. *Neuroimage*, *59*(1), 4–13.

Thornton, M. A., & Tamir, D. I. (2021a). People accurately predict the transition probabilities between actions. *Science Advances*, *7*, 1–12. https://doi.org/10.1126/sciadv.abd4995.

Thornton, M. A., & Tamir, D. I. (2021b). Perceiving actions before they happen: Psychological dimensions scaffold neural action prediction. *Social Cognitive and Affective Neuroscience*, *16*(8), 807–815.

Thornton, M. A., & Tamir, D. I. (2022). Six dimensions describe action understanding: The ACT-FASTaxonomy. *Journal of Personality and Social Psychology, 122*(4), 577–605.

Tomasello, M., Kruger, A. C., & Ratner, H. H. (1993). Cultural learning. *Behavioral and Brain Sciences, 16*(3), 495–511.

Troje, N. F., & Basbaum, A. (2008). Biological motion perception. *The Senses: A Comprehensive Reference, 2*, 231–238.

Tucciarelli, R., Wurm, M., Baccolo, E., & Lingnau, A. (2019). The representational space of observed actions. *elife, 8*, 1–24.

Turella, L., Pierno, A. C., Tubaldi, F., & Castiello, U. (2009). Mirror neurons in humans: Consisting or confounding evidence? *Brain and Language, 108*(1), 10–21.

Turella, L., Wurm, M. F., Tucciarelli, R., & Lingnau, A. (2013). Expertise in action observation: Recent neuroimaging findings and future perspectives. *Frontiers in Human Neuroscience, 7*, 1–5. https://doi.org/10.3389/fnhum.2013.00637.

Turella, L., Rumiati, R., & Lingnau, A. (2020). Hierarchical action encoding within the human brain. *Cerebral Cortex, 30*(5), 2924–2938. https://doi.org/10.1093/cercor/bhz284.

Uithol, S., van Rooij, I., Bekkering, H., & Haselager, P. (2012). Hierarchies in action and motor control. *Journal of Cognitive Neuroscience, 24*(5), 1077–1086.

Umiltà, M. A., Kohler, E., Gallese, V., et al. (2001). I know what you are doing: A neurophysiological study. *Neuron, 19*, 155–165.

Umiltà, M. A., Escola, L., Intskirveli, I., et al. (2008). When pliers become fingers in the monkey motor system. *Proceedings of the National Academy of Sciences, 105*(6), 2209–2213.

Ungerleider, L. G., & Mishkin, M. (1982). Two cortical visual systems. In *Analysis of Visual Behavior*. Edited by D. J. Ingle, M. A. Goodale, & R. J. W. Mansfield, 549–586. MIT Press.

Valentine, T., Lewis, M. B., & Hills, P. J. (2016). Face-space: A unifying concept in face recognition research. *Quarterly Journal of Experimental Psychology, 69*(10), 1996–2019.

Vallacher, R. R., & Wegner, D. M. (1989). Levels of personal agency: Individual variation in action identification. *Journal of Personality and Social Psychology, 57*, 660–671.

Van Overwalle, F. (2009). Social cognition and the brain: A meta-analysis. *Human Brain Mapping, 30*(3), 829–858.

Van Overwalle, F., & Baetens, K. (2009). Understanding others' actions and goals by mirror and mentalizing systems: A meta-analysis. *Neuroimage, 48*(3), 564–584.

Vannuscorps, G., & Caramazza, A. (2016). Typical action perception and interpretation without motor simulation. *Proceedings of the National Academy of Sciences, 113*(1), 86–91.

Vannuscorps, G., & Caramazza, A. (2023). Effector-specific motor simulation supplements core action recognition processes in adverse conditions. *Social Cognitive and Affective Neuroscience, 18*(1), 1–11.

Vinson, D. P., & Vigliocco, G. (2008). Semantic feature production norms for a large set of objects and events. *Behavior Research Methods, 40*(1), 183–190.

Vrigkas, M., Nikou, C., & Kakadiaris, I. A. (2015). A review of human activity recognition methods. *Frontiers in Robotics and AI, 2*, 1–28.

Watson, C. E., & Buxbaum, L. J. (2014). Uncovering the architecture of action semantics. *Journal of Experimental Psychology: Human Perception and Performance, 40*(5), 1832–1848.

Wilson, M., & Knoblich, G. (2005). The case for motor involvement in perceiving conspecifics. *Psychological Bulletin, 131*(3), 460–473.

Wurm, M. F., & Caramazza, A. (2019). Distinct roles of temporal and fronto-parietal cortex in representing actions across vision and language. *Nature Communications, 10*(1), 289.

Wurm, M. F., & Caramazza, A. (2022). Two 'what' pathways for action and object recognition. *Trends in Cognitive Sciences, 26*(2), 103–116.

Wurm, M. F., & Lingnau, A. (2015). Decoding actions at different levels of abstraction. *Journal of Neuroscience, 35*, 7727–7735.

Wurm, M. F., & Schubotz, R. I. (2012). Squeezing lemons in the bathroom: Contextual information modulates action recognition. *Neuroimage, 59*, 1551–1559.

Wurm, M. F., & Schubotz, R. I. (2017). What's she doing in the kitchen? Context helps when actions are hard to recognize. *Psychonomic Bulletin & Review, 24*, 503–509.

Wurm, M. F., Ariani, G., Greenlee, M., & Lingnau, A. (2015). Decoding concrete and abstract action representations during explicit and implicit conceptual processing. *Cerebral Cortex, 26*(8), 3390–3401. https://doi.org/10.1093/cercor/bhv169.

Wurm, M. F., Artemenko, C., Giuliani, D., & Schubotz, R. I. (2017a). Action at its place: Contextual settings enhance action recognition in 4- to 8-year-old children. *Developmental Psychology, 53*(4), 662–670.

Wurm, M. F., Caramazza, A., & Lingnau, A. (2017b). Action categories in lateral occipitotemporal cortex are organized along sociality and transitivity. *Journal of Neuroscience, 37*, 562–575.

Yau, J. M., Pasupathy, A., Brincat, S. L., & Connor, C. E. (2013). Curvature processing dynamics in macaque area V4. *Cerebral Cortex, 23*, 198–209.

Zacks, J. M., Speer, N. K., Swallow, K. M., Braver, T. S., & Reynolds, J. R. (2007). Event perception: A mind/brain perspective. *Psychological Bulletin, 133*(2), 273–293.

Zhuang, T., & Lingnau, A. (2022). The characterization of actions at the superordinate, basic and subordinate level. *Psychological Research, 86*(6), 1871–1891.

Zhuang, T., Kabulska, Z., & Lingnau, A. (2023). The representation of observed actions at the subordinate, basic and superordinate level. *Journal of Neuroscience, 43*(48), 8219–8230.

Acknowledgments

Our thanks to Jens Schwarzbach, Marius Zimmermann, Moritz Wurm, Deyan Mitev, Maximilian Reger, Marisa Birk, Federica Danaj, Zuzanna Kabulska, and Filip Djurovic for helpful discussions and comments on previous versions of this manuscript. A.L. was supported by a DFG Heisenberg-Professorship (LI 2840/2-1).

Cambridge Elements ☰

Perception

James T. Enns

The University of British Columbia

Editor James T. Enns is Professor at the University of British Columbia, where he researches the interaction of perception, attention, emotion, and social factors. He has previously been Editor of the *Journal of Experimental Psychology: Human Perception and Performance* and an Associate Editor at *Psychological Science, Consciousness and Cognition, Attention Perception & Psychophysics,* and *Visual Cognition.*

About the Series

The modern study of human perception includes event perception, bidirectional influences between perception and action, music, language, the integration of the senses, human action observation, and the important roles of emotion, motivation, and social factors. Each Element in the series combines authoritative literature reviews of foundational topics with forward-looking presentations of the recent developments on a given topic.

Cambridge Elements ☰

Perception

Printed in the United States
by Baker & Taylor Publisher Services